A FRESH APPROACH TO
ST JOHN OF THE CROSS

A fresh approach to

ST JOHN
OF THE CROSS

Ronald Rolheiser
Kevin Culligan
Richard Copsey
Ursula Fleming
Iain Matthew

edited by
John McGowan

ST PAULS

ST PAULS
Middlegreen, Slough SL3 6BT, United Kingdom
Moyglare Road, Maynooth, Co. Kildare, Ireland

© ST PAULS 1993

Cover by Graphic Examples

ISBN 085439 450 8

Printed by The Guernsey Press Co. Ltd, Guernsey, C.I.

ST PAULS is an activity of the priests and brothers of the Society
of St Paul who proclaim the Gospel through the media
of social communication

Contents

ABBREVIATIONS

A	=	Ascent of Mount Carmel; 1A first book, etc.
N	=	Dark Night of the Soul; 1N first book, etc.
F	=	Living Flame of Love (second redaction).
F°	=	F first redaction.
C	=	Spiritual Canticle (second redaction).
C°	=	C first redaction.
SLL	=	Sayings of Light and Love (Ruiz, Rodríguez numbering).
Lt	=	Letters (Ruiz, Rodríguez numbering).
R	=	Romances.

Single quotation marks, 'Canticle', denote the poem; underlining, *Canticle*, denotes the entire work.

P(A P...) = prologue to the respective work.

The man, the myth
and the truth

HISTORY AND MYTH

Some years ago, I attended a funeral of Belgian historian, Karel Blockx. The homilist at the funeral concluded by saying "Today we bury the man, now the myth begins!"

In the dark early hours of 13 December 1591, almost exactly five hundred years ago, John of the Cross died. With his burial, a myth began with which we have been contending ever since.

This essay, *John of the Cross – the man, the myth, and the truth*, will attempt to distinguish precisely between what was buried when John died five hundred years ago and what was born in the same moment. What happened when John died was similar to what happened when Jesus died: his followers created a hagiography, a myth, which, not unlike what great artists do to reality, heightened certain forms in his person at the cost of sacrificing a more accurate historical description. When scholars study Christ today, they make a distinction between the Jesus of history and the Christ of faith. When we study John of the Cross we must make a similar distinction. There is the John of the Cross of history and there is the John of the Cross of tradition and hagiography. This leaves us the problem of sorting out strict reality from myth.

In the literature and the circles of devotion and piety that have grown up around John these past four centuries, what is truth and what is myth? What was he really like? What is true to his person and what is the creation of conscious and unconscious hagiography?

Before examining those questions, it is useful to very briefly consider the reasons why a myth built up around him in the first place. Why did such a myth build up around John? Three factors conspired to help distort, for better and for worse, the image we have of him:

1. *A mystique builds up naturally around all people who radiate something extraordinary, be that positive or negative.* We spontaneously paint extraordinary people into saints, demons, weird characters, supermen, monsters, villains and the like. Every family, religious community, corporate or academic board room, and village or town abounds with stories about its characters. These stories are the stuff of myth. To create them, we, not unlike artists, accentuate certain forms by deliberately distorting and exaggerating them, rather than photographically copying them or journalistically reporting them, in order to highlight and bring out an essence. This exaggeration of form to highlight essence lies at the base of myth.

This has been very operative in the way John has been treated through the centuries by admirers and critics alike. What they exaggerate about John we will see later. Suffice it here to say that the picture they have handed us of John of the Cross is as much mythical as it is historical.

2. *John's mythology has been very much shaped by well-intentioned, but bad, biography.* Today we no longer understand how they used to write biography. Our bias is for history in a stricter sense. We enjoy biography but, when we write biographies, our attempt is to be as critical and factual as possible. Our approach is more that of the journalist than the artist. For us, the truest biography would be a video tape-recording of some-

one's life. This itch for the factual over the essential is, however, recent in history. Up to a few decades ago, especially in biographies of persons we considered saintly, the idea was much more to glorify and deify them than to present the strict facts. Biography was really hagiography; a certain iconography even. When authors wrote lives of saints, they consciously and unconsciously distorted and exaggerated history to highlight soul. For example, Nikos Kazantzakis begins his biography of Francis of Assisi by stating explicitly that his concern is not with historical fact and that he will change and distort fact to bring out the essence of Francis. His attempt is more to draw a picture of Francis' soul than to give a documentary-type video tape of his life. This is deliberate hagiography and Kazantzakis does it well. Until recently, almost all lives of the saints were done within this literary genre. And, as is the case still with contemporary biography, some writers were good and others were awful.

John of the Cross has been subjected to more than his share of biography by the latter. This has helped perpetrate and perpetuate a distorted image of him. However, because we no longer understand the intent of hagiography, and tend to read writings in this genre in a literal sense, even good biographies of him have helped to distort his image. Simply put, past writers were trying to paint us a picture of his soul (and art, by definition, exaggerates form) and we have tended to see that art as a photograph. The result has led to a very harmful distortion.

3. *Finally, John, because of the way he wrote, did not help his own cause.* It is not easy to read John and understand what he was actually saying and most people who read him end up misunderstanding him. This adds to the myth. John's writings are so complex that he would need his own hermeneutical textbook for interpretation.

He freely mixes a number of literary genres and, unless his reader is sensitive to every shift in literary mode, his reader is likely to misunderstand.

John, is first and foremost, a poet. Hence, always in his writings, we are dealing with images and metaphors. He is ever the artist, painting reality rather than reporting it as a journalist. He is not a journalist and when we read his writings as we would a newspaper, they often seem overwhelming, negative and masochistic. Reading John of the Cross correctly is more like going to an art museum than it is like reading the daily paper. Unfortunately, he has, too often, been read as one reads the daily paper. His myth partly arises out of that.

Beyond his propensity for poetic images, John, who was a scholar of Aristotle, is fond of using distinctions and language found only in Greek philosophy. He presupposes his reader understands Aristotle and his metaphysics, coupled with the fact that he is writing for professional contemplatives, Carmelite nuns well along in the spiritual life (whom he, to the confusion of to-day's reader, calls 'beginners') obfuscates things even more.

Moreover, his works are pieces of extraordinary subtlety demanding, for proper understanding, a rare capacity to hold certain polarities in a delicate balance. This capacity for paradox, for subtle differentiation and fine distinction, which you see in all great thinkers, often cannot be sustained by the followers of those same thinkers. Invariably the disciple is not as great as the master, particularly regarding the master's capacity to think in shades of grey rather than in simple blacks and whites. John's followers have, far too often, been unable to grasp and hold in proper balance the central aspects of his thought, especially as these pertain to suffering and joy. Consequently, a myth has grown up around him, among both admirers and critics alike, which has, as we will see, made him out to be rather inhuman and the perpetrator of a spirituality which is only for certain mystical and ascetical athletes.

Given all of this, what does the mythical John of the Cross look like?

JOHN OF THE CROSS OF HAGIOGRAPHY... THE MYSTIC OF POPULAR PIETY

A generalisation is never completely accurate, but, often times, has immense value because, in it, vast amounts of material are seen within one synthetic block. Admitting the limitation of this generalisation (and submitting that, in any case, even scientific theories are under subscribed), let me risk painting a picture of the John of the Cross of hagiography, the myth of John.

By both his admirers and his critics alike, John of the Cross is often understood this way:

He is a brilliant person, whatever his faults. However, he is, ultimately, a most austere, severe, ascetical and inhuman person, someone who is insensitive to the normal feelings, urges and distractions that incurably haunt the rest of us. He is pathologically single-minded, not given to any nonsense, distractions or humour. He is heavy, the mystic of darkness, suffering and the cross. He's deep, that we admit, but scary too! Despite this depth, he, in the end, lacks balance. He is a spiritual masochist, counselling us to choose always pain over pleasure, what is more difficult over what is more pleasant, and life after death over life after birth. As well, his system comes from his mysticism, namely, from some extraordinary revelations from God which are the prerogative of certain spiritual athletes like himself and other great mystics. These mystical revelations are themselves a sign that he is divorced from the bread and butter of life (not your average neighbour whom you invite over on a Sunday evening for drinks and a barbecue!) He's a saint, but, in the end, he and his spirituality do not enter with true understanding the realm of ordinary day-to-day life, with all its heartaches and headaches over relationships, mortgages, money, sex, careers, food and entertainment. He is a great man, one in a million, and his books are great books, but his person is divorced from the ordinary person and his spirituality is a high road for a religious elite.

In the end, for the most part, both his admirers and critics, despite gracious or begrudged admiration for him, do not really believe that John of the Cross understands them within their real lives and struggles nor that his spirituality offers them empathy and practical guidance. He is distant, like some beautiful, but remote, art object... something you stare at and perhaps even admire, but that you go home from!

Soren Kierkegaard once said of Christ: "What Christ wants is not admirers but followers." The myth that now surrounds John of the Cross and his works has, unfortunately, stigmatised John in the same way. He still has his admirers, but these, for the main part, consider his person and teaching as something too elitist, heavy, fixated on the cross and suffering, and too otherworldly to help them concretely in their ordinary lives.

As long as this particular myth, the John of the Cross of hagiography, survives, John and his works will always be considered by the popular mind as exotic, elitist, unhealthily fixated on the cross and the next life, and as too unordinary to act as a guide for the average full-blooded person.

But... this is the myth of John of the Cross. This is the John of the Cross of bad biographies and bad reading. What is the real John of the Cross like and what do he and his writings offer to the full-blooded person?

To understand who John of the Cross truly is and what his writings really offer, it is helpful to situate his person and his writings against a four-fold backdrop:

1. Eros lies at the deep heart of his person and his spirituality

John of the Cross was the child of Romeo and Juliet. He was a love-child, conceived of a passion so powerful that his father willingly renounced his family and their rather substantial wealth, privilege and status to marry a peasant woman for whom he felt a love so strong that nothing else mattered other than consummation and a community of life with her. John was the child of that union, in every way. At the root of his personality and all his works lies this passion, this eros, this single-mindedness, this capacity to renounce all else, to truly leave father and mother and lands, for that one great love.

He was a lover, and his spirituality is incomprehensible when that is not seen as its root dynamism. His famous poem, *The Ascent of Mount Carmel*, better known as *The Dark Night of the Soul*, begins with the words: "One dark night, fired by love's urgent longings." The urgent longings he is speaking about here are what drove his father to forsake all in order to be with the woman he married. They are the same longings that drove John, throughout his life, from transformation through transformation, to union with his beloved, the body of Christ.

To understand John, one must understand this passion. His temperament showed his breeding... he was the child of Romeo and Juliet. He was full-blooded and his is a spirituality for the full-blooded in a way that very few spiritualities can ever approximate.

2. He was a natural mystic

This is the most critical factor in understanding John. Just as the great artist or intellectual is, in the end, the product of nature and not first of all of intense effort, so too is the great mystic. Great mystics, as is the case with artists and intellectuals, are born not made. What is important about this is that, just as the great artist or intellectual is somewhat, by nature and charism, pathologically single-minded about his or her natural area of interest, so too is the mystic.

However, in order to understand more fully what this means and how it impacts our understanding of John of the Cross, it is necessary to, first of all, discuss at some length the concepts of mysticism and mystic.

What is mysticism? Few words are as commonly misunderstood, misused and maligned as is the word mysticism. Briefly stated, mysticism is being touched by God in a deep inchoate way, that is, in a way that is both revelatory and authoritative, but is beyond what can be adequately conceptualised, felt or articulated. This caption-type definition draws upon two sets of distinctions:

A distinction among the various ways someone can be in union and communion with another

When one analyses how one can communicate with another and be in union with him or her, it is profitable to differentiate among four levels:

(i) The verbal: We reach each other and communicate through words, speech;

(ii) The bodily: We all know that, at times, our bodies speak more honestly and more clearly than our words.

The language of our bodies (anger, tension, rigidity, frigidity, nervousness, ease) often touches others and speaks to them more deeply than does our speech. It is harder to lie with our bodies than with our words.

(iii) The ritual: Beyond the power of words and body language, we have too the power to reach each other, and deeply, through ritual language. When our words and our bodies no longer have the power to reach another, we can have recourse to ritual language, namely, ritual gestures that touch others and communicate something to them that the spoken word and the body (divorced from ritual symbol) cannot do. For example, imagine going to a funeral and trying to console someone whom you love. At such an occasion, there are no words that are ultimately very helpful, nor can you, just by being there and having your body radiate sympathy, enter very deeply into empathy with the one who is mourning a loved one. At such a time, you resort to ritual language. The most timeless and primal ritual of all time is the ritual of the embrace. You go up to your friend and you embrace him or her. Nothing need be said and, in fact, words often get in the way of true communication at such times. The embrace is what communicates what you really want to say. Your friend is touched in a way deeper than can be achieved through words and body language.

Note how, as one descends these levels from words to body language, to ritual, the touch is ever more inchoate – the communication and unity is ever more ineffable, dark and less available for imaginative, cognitive and even affective analysis.

(iv) The mystical: However, we can touch each other and lie inside of each other in a way that is even deeper than the unity brought about by words, body language and ritual gesture. Sometimes our deepest communication takes place outside of these. Sometimes we know that we are connected at a deeper level. We spontaneously name this unity in various ways: soul-mate, moral affinity, con-naturality, karma and mysticism, among other names. This is the level of mysticism precisely because a mystique is present in the communication and union. We are in connection with someone in a way that goes beyond what is explicable in terms of verbal, bodily, ritual and even intuitive communication.

Mysticism is then, as we saw, a deep but inchoate experience of union with someone. More specifically, the word is used to describe this kind of union with God. By definition, it is an experience which befuddles somewhat language, the mind and even the heart. That is why classical mystics so often use the word 'dark' when speaking of this kind of experience.

What is important to highlight in this analysis is that mysticism is an ordinary experience. Like spoken, bodily and ritual communication it is an ordinary everyday experience for everyone.

A distinction among various faculties within us

Mediaeval philosophy used to make a distinction which, today, finds an echo in circles of pop psychology:

(i) The intellect (the head): This is our thinking centre from which issues forth our rationality.

(ii) The will (the heart): This is our feeling centre from which issue forth our passions and emotions.

(iii) The memory (the gut): This is neither a centre of thought nor of feelings in the sense of affective or emotional feeling. The gut is the centre where we are touched, and very deeply, in a way that is precisely beyond words, rational thought and emotions. It might perhaps be described as our 'ought' centre. It is the place inside of us where, inchoately, we sense certain dictates, things that we ought to do. It is like a religious and moral brand inside of us. At its worst it is experienced as an obsession or a compulsion; at its best, it is mysticism. This centre touches both the head and heart, but in a dark way. As John of the Cross himself says, it rests "upon nothing of what one understands, tastes, feels or imagines. All these perceptions are a darkness... (it) lies beyond this understanding, taste, feeling and imagining" (*The Ascent to Mount Carmel*, Book 1, Chapter 13, no. 11 and Book 2, Chapter 4, no. 2).

Mysticism lies mainly at the level of the gut. Irrespective of the rather terrible aesthetics of the word, it is in the gut that there is true mystique, where we are strangely and powerfully drawn to where, as John says, "we understand more by not understanding than by understanding" (*The Living Flame of Love*, Stanza 3, no. 48).

Again, as in the previous set of distinctions, it is important to see that the experience of mysticism is very ordinary, normal, an everyday experience. In a sense, it is the extraordinary experience of the ordinary person – an experience which, while powerful, morally non-negotiable and morally binding, befuddles the ordinary self-reflective logic of the head and heart. And it is, in the end, the experience of being in unity with something; specifically, in union with God.

Given the ordinariness of mysticism, does this make us all mystics? No. Mysticism is common and everyday; mystics are not. What is the difference?

Most persons, to paraphrase Ruth Burrows, have mystical experience but have it "light off". The mystic has the same experience but he or she has it "light on". What makes someone a mystic, therefore, is that he or she can give a certain expression, however inadequate, to what is happening dynamically at that deep inchoate level. The mystic is to the religious realm what the artist is to the aesthetic one. Everyone has deep aesthetic experiences but only the artist can give to them some kind of proper expression. Everyone has mystical experiences but only the mystic can give them some kind of fitting expression. The artist and the mystic thus also play similar roles in their respective communities. By attempting to give expression to that which is beyond adequate expression, they help sensitise the larger community to what it is actually experiencing.

And now to our point: the artist and the mystic also have similar origins and obsessions. Great artists and great mystics are born. They are gifted that way primarily by nature rather than effort. In both cases, normally they are also somewhat obsessed by their gift. Little in life can distract them for long from a non-negotiable *vocatio* that they feel. Soren Kierkegaard, once defined a saint as someone who "wills the one thing". Not all great mystics and artists are saints because they do not necessarily will *the* one thing, but all *will one thing*. All are pathologically single-minded.

One must understand this in order to relate properly to John of the Cross' personality and his works. John, much like Teilhard de Chardin in our own century, was born a mystic. He was naturally obsessed with God, and his pathological single-mindedness comes from that. When his myth accuses him of not being ordinary and full-blooded, it does so only because it misses this crucial point. He was pathologically full-blooded and the experiences he writes about are, in the end, ordinary experiences open to all of us. What was not ordinary about him was his greatness. His personality and works are not exotic and weird. They are simply characterised and marked by all the qualities of the great mystic. He was not ordinary but the intimidation we feel from him and his works is the same intimidation that the amateur musician feels when listening to and examining the works of great composers such as Mozart, Handel or Bach. They are frightening to us amateurs because they are out of our league, not because their music is frightening. On the contrary, their music is beautiful. John of the Cross is often seen as this distant, obsessed, inhuman figure for precisely this reason

3. He was concerned for structural transformation

The myth of John presents him as an unbalanced ascetic and a spiritual masochist, someone obsessed with the cross, suffering and the heavy parts of the gospel. This too is a misunderstanding. In the end, John is obsessed with consummation, joy and play, the wedding banquet and marriage bed as Christ describes them.

If this is true, then why are his books so severe and so focused on the paschal mystery?

Given what we just saw, the impatient erotic character that he inherited by being the child of Romeo and Juliet and the strongly obsessional nature that he had as a natural mystic, it is logical that he would be restless for depth, and impatient with anything that delays or distracts one from union with one's beloved. Hence his proclivity for structural transformation over lesser types of transformation and his itch to remain focused on the central mystery of transformation within our Christian faith, the paschal mystery.

More simply put, when you are an incurable romantic by nature and are obsessively in love, you do not want to waste a lot of time in things that will distract you from your wedding bed. You want to get on with pursuing the consummation, irrespective of the renunciations this will mean. When John looked at the gospels, he correctly understood that only by being radically transformed (*structurally* transformed, in psychological terminology) can we come to that marriage bed: "unless the grain of wheat falls into the ground and dies, it cannot come to eternal life." There is no final and full life without first there being a Good Friday. The pattern of Christ's passion-death-resurrection-ascension-Pentecost (undergoing the 'dark night of the soul') is the way to the consummation, ecstasy, restfulness, play and joy that will finally let our erotic hearts rest in peace. John was focused so heavily on the cross only because it is the means to get us to the consummation of the true marriage bed. He is not a masochist but an eroticist; he is not hung up on suffering but on consummation; he is not fixated on Good Friday but is impatient for Easter Sunday. A careful examination of his personality and his writings reveals this without equivocation.

4. He wrote all his works for professional religious in whom he presupposed initial conversion.

Many of the confusions that surround John of the Cross clarify when one places his life's ministry and his written works within their proper context. John spent his life trying to reform contemplative religious life, particularly among his Carmelite male brethren. He penned his works mainly as guides for the prayer life of professed religious within contemplative orders. When this is considered, many things in his writings which seem abrasive, unbalanced and even masochistic become more palatable.

Two things in particular need highlighting here:

(i) Because his supposed audience was normally professed religious living in contemplative convents or monasteries, he links all movements within transformation (the passage through dark night of the soul) to prayer and to one's fidelity to it and its various stages and methods. This perspective, looked at by someone who is outside the walls of a contemplative religious order, seems dangerously weak vis-a-vis the dimensions of social justice and human relationships. This, as we will see, is again a misreading, a bad hermeneutical rendering of his works. For a contemplative monk or nun, one's prayer life is one's central relationship, duty of state and outreach in the area of social justice. Moreover, the dynamics of prayer, the natural transformation that will occur if one prays honestly and regularly, are, as we shall see, the same dynamics that one finds in relationships and in social justice work or in any ministry or service whatever. John was writing to professional contemplatives. He traces out what they should do and what they should expect will happen to them by using the dynamics inherent in formal prayer. Had he been writing to any other group of persons (married couple, social justice advocates, missionaries, teachers, housewives, politicians) he would have ultimately said exactly the same thing, though in a different language. The fact that he used the language surrounding prayer, and traces out its dynamics to describe how structural transformation occurs is accidental and incidental. Unfortunately this is rarely seen and understood and, hence, his spirituality is often seen as unbalanced, privatised, elitist and unrealistic for someone living in the world.

(ii) The fact that John is writing for vowed contemplative nuns and monks accounts too for another major misunderstanding.

There is a leitmotif in his writings wherein one hears regularly the refrain: "You should be separated from the world; you should avoid the world's distractions; and you should, even in the monastery or convent, not be a socialite. Withdrawal is the surest way to God." When this refrain is taken as counsel for anyone who is not a religious within a contemplative order, it betrays an attitude towards the world and towards human community which is not at all Christian and is dangerously unhealthy. However, John was not offering this as counsel for persons who are not inside contemplative walls. For someone outside those walls, his or her relationships, duties of state and work then functionally substitute for many of the dynamics that would, for the professional contemplative who has withdrawn from the world, take place through withdrawal and formal prayer. Thus, for example, a mother at home with young children finds herself in a very real desert, withdrawn from the world. For those outside of contemplative convents and monasteries, there is in their duties of state an in-built asceticism that, if lived out properly, more than adequately provides many of the dynamics that one finds within monastery walls. Again, a proper reading of John reveals this.

Rarely is John of the Cross examined against this backdrop. This explains why he is rarely properly understood.

What was he really like? What kind of man lurks behind the myth?

The Greek philosophical tradition of Socrates, Plato and Aristotle believed that, as human beings, we are fired into life with a madness that comes from the gods and which makes us incurably restless for a great love, for the perpetuation of our own seed, and to contemplate the divine.

Few phrases are as apt to describe John of the Cross. He was a man of great eros and passion, driven towards attaining the great love; he was a man of great artistic ability, driven towards perpetuating himself in some great creation; and he was the natural mystic, obsessed with contemplating the divine.

We can picture him then, the child of Romeo and Juliet, the natural mystic, restless, with high energy, bright, creative, impatient, single-minded, obsessed, driven towards attaining the great love. He, ever acutely aware that in this life all symphonies remain unfinished, is then understandably obsessed with depth, with whatever offers a route towards great love, immortality and permanent union with God, other and the world. That makes him impatient with distractions. Understandably he becomes a monk, and a contemplative one. He is often impatient with those within his own community who are less pilgrim of soul. He becomes friends with those whom he senses as soul-mates. Teresa of Avila becomes his friend and co-conspirator. He, like a lover looking forward to the consummation of the wedding night, becomes impatient with life itself and "laments that a life so weak and base impedes another so mighty and sublime" (*Living Flame*, Stanza 1, no. 31).

His complexity befuddles us. His sharp mind demands that the heart and gut obey it, even as he writes from the heart and tells us that love is more important than thought. However, in all of this, he is clear that in the end the gut, our mystical centre, is the truest indicator of God's voice. It must be obeyed... its compulsions are our liberation.

Under girding all of this, his contemporaries assure us, was a man of gentleness and deep charity who, while novice master, got into trouble for taking his novices out on too many picnics, and who constantly taught that play is the ultimate goal of the spiritual life.

A MASTER OF SOUL CRAFT

Samuel Butler once distinguished between what he called 'statecraft' and 'soul craft'. In his mind, both are needed to come to wholeness and community.

Statecraft is the art of creating community among people. It combines sociology, politics, justice concerns, institutional structures and religious insight. Soul craft is the art of shaping the soul, channelling eros and ordering the mind, heart and gut correctly. It combines psychology, physiology and religious insight.

John of the Cross is one the great masters of all time of the art of soul craft. What John offers in this realm is parallel to what a Mozart offers in the area of music, a Michelangelo offers in the area of painting and sculpture, and what a Shakespeare offers in the area of literature. He is a master and what he produced is, in a manner of speaking, the purest of the pure. It can seem elitist and intimidating to the amateur for that reason.

George Eliot once wrote a book entitled, *The Lifted Veil*. In it he tells the story of a woman who had extraordinary psychic powers. She could see into the future because, for her, the veil of time had been lifted. Looking into the future, she saw many things, some of which frightened her quite badly.

John of the Cross is a master of soul craft because, for him, the veil was also partially lifted. As a great mystic, he was not given insights into the future but he was given privileged insight into the dynamics of love, prayer, transformation, suffering and consummation. His books might also aptly be entitled, *The Lifted Veil*. Only a person for whom the veil has been partially lifted can articulate soul craft of the following kind:

To reach satisfaction in all
desire its possession in nothing.
To come to possess all
desire the possession of nothing.
To arrive at being all
desire to be nothing.
To come to the knowledge of all
desire the knowledge of nothing.
To come to the pleasure you have not
you must go by a way in which you enjoy not.

To come to the knowledge you have not
you must go by a way in which you know not.
To come to the possession you have not
you must go by a way in which you possess not.
To come to be what you are not
you must go by a way in which you are not.
When you turn towards something
you cease to cast yourself upon the all.
For to go from all to all
you must deny yourself of all in all.
And when you come to the possession of the all
you must possess it without wanting anything.
Because if you desire to have something in all
your treasure in God is not purely your all.
In this nakedness the spirit finds
its quietude and rest.
For in coveting nothing,
nothing raises it up
and nothing weighs it down,
because it is in the centre of its humility.
When it covets something
in this very desire it is wearied.

> (*The Ascent to Mount Carmel*,
> Book 1, Chapter 13, no. 11)

Given this, we see that, while his person and his writings are somewhat beyond the ordinary, his spirituality is not elitist, a high road for spiritual athletes. Shakespeare was a one-in-a-million writer but his plays are meant to be enjoyed by the millions. John of the Cross was a one-in-a-million mystic but his works are meant to give insight and challenge to the millions. The common folk enjoy the Mozarts, Michelangelos, and Shakespeares... even as they know that these were not ordinary composers, artists and writers. They were rare, great geniuses who gave a precious expression to ordinary experience.

John of the Cross, once the myth is excised from the reality, should be understood in the same way. He is a rare, great genius, a one-in-a-million master of soul craft, who gave precious expression to ordinary religious experience.

Ronald Rolheiser

John
and human development

THE DARK NIGHT OF THE SOUL...
A CONTEMPORARY INTERPRETATION

The theme adds John's contribution to a popular theme today. It shows that John was not a dualist, caring only for the spiritual part of a person; he recognised the value of human growth on every level, beginning with the emotional-psychological.

SOME NECESSARY FOCUSING

When John of the Cross speaks of the dark night of the soul, he is speaking of a purifying passage that an individual undergoes which transforms one kind of life into another. In a simplistic manner of speaking, natural life becomes eschatological life, earthly life becomes eternal life, and life which draws its support from natural gratification becomes life that draws its support from the motivation of Christ. In metaphorical terms, what happens in a dark night of the soul is that the grain of wheat falls into the ground and dies so that it can give birth to new life.

Almost universally, this transformation, as articulated by John, is understood as something that pertains mostly to prayer. Too infrequently is it understood as something that has to do with our entire lives... relationships, work and play. However, what John describes in his concept of the dark night of the soul is really the paschal mystery, the movement through death from Good Friday to Easter Sunday. This movement has to do with the transformation of our whole lives. John's outline of this can, therefore, serve as a paradigm of paschal transformation ("structural" transformation, in the terminology of certain current schools of psychology). The dark night of the soul traces the pattern that love, service and prayer must move through to come to eternal life.

Two common misunderstandings of John must first be dispelled before this becomes more clear:

1. All too common is the idea that John was a spiritual masochist, unhealthily fixed upon suffering and the cross, preferring Good Friday to Easter Sunday. This is false. John was a natural mystic and, as such, was by temperament very single-minded (not unlike great artists and great writers who are, too, in a similar fashion focused in a way that can to an outsider appear obsessive). This single-mindedness made him impatient for the unity and consummation promised in the kingdom, and impatient with anything that delays this. Hence, given this, it is understandable that he will, without much patience with anything else, zero-in on the mystery of how suffering and dying bring forth eternal life. He knows that resurrection comes after suffering and death and, since he is impatient for Easter Sunday, his focus is on Good Friday.

2. Common too is the conception that John's spirituality, since it outlines the dynamics of transformation through tracing out the inner dynamics of prayer, is narrow, privatised and elitist; at best, of use and interest to monks and nuns and other such contemplatives. John speaks explicitly of the transformation of prayer (and much less directly of the transformation of our love relationships and our lives of service) and he sees the end of the process of transformation primarily as union with God (and not so much union within human community). The elements of community and justice appear to be quite weak in his system.

This, however, requires a closer look. When his system is dissected more closely, as this article will attempt to do, the dynamics for transformation that he outlines for our prayer lives can be seen to have a near perfect parallel in our love lives and in our lives of service and justice. John wrote his commentaries primarily with professional contemplatives in mind, people whose primary 'job' it was to pray and whose primary relationship in this life was a mystical and vertical one to God. In the case of his historical audience, their primary duty of state (moral and practical responsibility) was formal prayer. John submits that in the proper evolution of prayer, in its transformation, there would occur a wider transformation in one's entire life. John knew his audience, professional contemplatives, and wrote accordingly. Had he been writing to another audience, one whose primary duty of state would have been to relate in the world, raise children and work for justice, he would have used a very different language... without however changing in any way the principles of transformation that he enunciates.

What he articulates in his concept of the dark night of the soul are the inner dynamics of paschal transformation, dynamics that apply in an identical way to the growth and transformation of our relationships, our love lives, and our lives of service in the world. His idea is that if you undergo a true dark night in any one of these, you will, in a manner of speaking, pull the others along with you. Thus, if one undergoes a true transformation in her life of prayer, her life of love and service will be similarly transformed. Conversely, to undergo a true transformation in one's love life will bring with it a true transformation of one's prayer life and life of service as well. The dynamics are the same. The paradigm is the same. A dark night is about the transformation of prayer, love and service to others, albeit John articulates it explicitly only as it pertains to prayer.

As well, the resurrection that is achieved at the end of a dark night of the soul puts one into deeper union with God... as well as with one's fellow human beings and with cosmic nature. Hence, what John traces out for us with his concept of the dark night of the soul is a paradigm for paschal transformation vis-a-vis all aspects of our lives and is a pattern for unity with God, human community and nature.

What is this paradigm for transformation? What are its stages?

JOHN'S PARADIGM OF THE DARK NIGHT OF THE SOUL. SIX STAGES IN THE TRANSFORMATION OF PRAYER, RELATIONSHIP AND SERVICE

1. A synthetic outline of the stages of growth and transformation

In John's view there are six stages one passes through in the paschal passage from death to life. These apply in an identical way to prayer, love and service:

(i) Pre-Conversion – 'Indifference'

In this stage, four things are manifest in one's life: lack of focus, unhealthy indifference, unchannelled eros, and gratification as the primary motivation for one's actions.

In brief, prior to conversion, one goes through life with an unhealthy indifference (and, as contemporary psychology has rightly pointed out, indifference, not hatred is the opposite of love).

At this stage, one feels one's eros deeply, but one lacks clear direction. Love can be, and often is, fairly promiscuous. In a contemporary colloquialism, one 'hangs loose' and loves what he or she is attracted to at the moment, especially what brings pleasure. Choices and commitments are made, ultimately, on the basis of what gratifies the self. In this stage, there is no true commitment, no true virtue and no real giving of the self to anything beyond itself. However sophisticated and altruistically disguised an action may look, in the end one is 'doing one's own thing'. Narcissism, egoism and the idiosyncratic preference lie at the basis of every moral action.

At this stage, no real prayer, love or service of others is possible, even though the person may be under a powerful illusion that he or she is genuinely praying or loving.

(ii) *Conversion – 'Falling in Love'*
   (*'The active night of the senses'*)

Iris Murdoch says, "the world can change in 15 seconds." The novelist, Morris West, says, "all conversion begins with the act of falling in love." Both are right.

Indifference is overcome by falling in love and, with that, immediately lives change. Three things then characterise a life: focus, the loss of indifference, and a change in what fuels motivation so that, in one way, a person can act beyond his or her own gratification.

Conversion begins with falling in love, with either a person, God, or with some principle, ideal or ideology. With that 'falling in love' comes the immediate loss of indifference. Instead there is a clear focus, one no longer "hangs loose". In fact, very often one becomes obsessed with what one loves to the point of losing one's freedom. This brings with it, at one level at least, a new motivation. There is, to a point, a movement beyond the self, beyond the pleasure-principle in its more infantile form. At one level, that which pertains to the person or object loved, one can become quite self-sacrificing, even to the point of giving up one's life for the beloved. In this is present the initial act of conversion.

(iii)*First fervour* – *'The honeymoon'*
('The active night of the senses comes to full bloom')

Following the initial moment of conversion, the moment of falling in love, almost invariably a person goes through a season characterised by something John calls 'first fervour'.

While in the first fervour, one's life is coloured by six things: high levels of feeling, desire and passion; the desire for greatness and uniqueness; excess in the area that pertains to one's love; endless energy, especially in the areas that pertain to one's love; public display to the world regarding one's love; and discursive abilities towards and regarding one's love.

What all this means will become clearer through the examples given later. In brief, however, during this period, the person acts exactly as one acts when one is on a honeymoon with one's ultimate love... one feels a passion that relativises all other loves, past and present; one has the sense that this love is the most unique, poetic and special love that has ever occurred in history (and that he or she is now also most unique and special because of it); there is the tendency constantly to excess (one cannot get enough of the beloved, nothing is too much); the love is a great energiser and long hours and endless demands appear as nothing; there is a great desire for public display (to let the world know that one has found this love); and there is the deep and constant desire to talk to the loved one or, barring that, to talk to others about the loved one.

(iv)*Waning of fervour* – *'The death of the honeymoon'*
(The passive night of the senses)

All honeymoons, given sufficient time, die. All fervour, given time, wanes. With this 'death', John tell us, one's life, especially as it relates to its beloved (but also in general) is characterised by five things: disillusionment, the loss of passion and consolation; boredom; the loss of the desire to talk to and about the loved one; and a growing solicitousness about the loved one.

All honeymoons eventually end. That is simply a fact of experience. What experience also teaches is what kind of feelings then characterise our lives. When the initial fervour of love dies, it is followed by a certain disillusionment, a loss of passion and desire, and a certain boredom with the one who formerly seemed the answer to one's every restless desire. With that comes a certain reticence vis-a-vis talking to or about the loved one. All of this can, and often times does, appear most confusing to the person. There is a certain disappointment, a feeling of having lost something very important, coupled, almost always, with the desire to do things that will bring back the fervour of the honeymoon.

That all honeymoons end is a fact of experience. What is less obvious is why this must always happen.

In some cases, honeymoons end because of infidelity and lack of interest, a person falls in love with someone else or simply loses interest in the one he or she formerly loved so passionately. This, while it produces almost the identical symptoms that mark a genuine dark night of the soul, is not a dark night in John's understanding of things. For John this is then a case of psychological depression brought on by infidelity. One knows it is not a genuine dark night because, in the case of infidelity, the characteristic of a growing solicitousness about the beloved will not be present. Instead the focus of the person who is experiencing the disillusionment, boredom, loss of passion and loss of the discursive ability, will be much more narcissistic, that is, turned in on himself or herself. In such a case, the honeymoon died, not because one has begun to lose his or her conversion. (John, in a passage which is perhaps the singularly most used passage in all his writings, *The Dark Night of the Soul*, Book 1, Chapter 9, outlines some very penetrating and useful criteria to discern a true dark night from a false one.)

However, in John's view, even if one remains faithful, one's honeymoon will end in any case. All initial fervour eventually dies and a disillusionment, loss of passion, boredom and the loss of discursiveness towards and about one's beloved replace the passion of the honeymoon. Why?

In John's view, God actively ends the honeymoon. God "dries up the fervour" and God does this not because God is masochistic or unwilling to let us live in pleasure for long. No. God ends the honeymoon because, up to this point, the one in love has not really been in love with what he perceives as his beloved (God, another person, the poor, some moral principle). He has, up to this point, been in love *with the experience itself*, the experience of being in love, of praying, of serving the poor, or whatever. The honeymoon ends so that he can come face-to-face with the person behind the experience of prayer, love or service. Only after a honeymoon ends does one find out whether or not he is really interested in somebody else (God, another person, the poor) or whether he is mostly interested in how relating to that person makes him feel.

In this waning of fervour, the passive night of the senses in John's terminology, one is given the chance to begin to actually relate to his loved one, beyond the experience that love itself has generated. In the waning of fervour, one finds out whether he is actually interested in God or only in the experience of praying; whether he is actually interested in a certain person or only in the experience of being in love; and whether he is interested in serving the poor, or in certain moral principles, or whether he is only interested in the feeling he gets in being involved with the poor and/or certain moral principles. Hopefully, the illustrations, given in the next section will help make this clear.

(v) *Proficiency* – *'The growth of easefulness'*

In John's view, the movement from stage to stage within this paschal process is ultimately an organic one. Certain growth naturally leads to a new phase of life. Thus, falling in love leads to a honeymoon, which leads to a deep bonding, which leads beyond the experience itself to the person behind it. Given all this, there is a certain inherent logic in movement to the next stage, proficiency.

This stage is characterised by three things which build upon each other: decision, dryness and ease. Proficiency is entered into when one makes a decision for something for its own sake, as opposed to deciding for it for some reason of narcissism and self-interest. This will be followed by dryness, a stage within which one feels little or no psychological or emotional consolation in relationship to her loved person or cause. However, if one perseveres in fidelity to that person or cause, John submits that, eventually, one begins to feel a certain ease and loving attentiveness, in relationship to her beloved. In its presence, she begins to feel not the passion of the honeymoon but a deep sense of being 'at home'.

For John, proficiency is already a high development within one's spiritual journey; one is already through a major phase (the dark night of the senses) in the journey of paschal transformation. There has already been a falling in the ground and dying in order to come to eternal life. At this stage, a major blockage has been removed... one can stay at this level for many years, or one can, from it, make the final and most dramatic leap of faith.

41

(vi) *The Final Stage of Growth Towards Transformation* *–'The Purification of One's Guidance System'* *(The dark night of the spirit)*

There are two major phases in this last stage, each with a different feeling. John calls these two phases "the active and the passive night of the spirit" and the "experience of the living flame". The former phase is characterised by a raging desolation, and the latter by a joyous passion and intermittent ecstasies.

For John, relatively few persons, in fact, enter this final stage, and an even fewer number complete it. To have completed this phase is to have attained all the purification necessary for the life of heaven. Full sainthood, complete with some of the ecstasy of heaven, is what lies at the end of this final stage.

It begins when, after a certain period of proficiency, a person makes a radical decision to live by faith alone. In essence, a person decides to live and act according to the written dictates of the Christian creeds and Scriptures, even when this goes radically against what her head and heart and friends suggest as being practical and spiritual wisdom. At this stage, a person truly radicalises regarding her discipleship in Christ and nothing that she can "see, feel, think, touch, taste, or sense" alters what she sees as commanded of her through the written dictates of Christ and the Church. In a manner of speaking, at this stage, one becomes 'fundamentalistic' in the good sense. The written word of Scripture cuts real life and it, without the usual nuances that come from common sense and practical wisdom, determines what is wise and what is to be done.

Immediately after making such a decision, the easefulness of proficiency dissolves and one enters a period of fierce disconsolate dryness. For John, this is by far the most painful part of the whole journey of purification. In this period, the person is habitually disconsolate and in interior pain. This is the fullest experience of 'Good Friday' given us in this life. Strangely though, not unlike Paul's experience in 2 Corinthians 4, even as one feels one's outer world completely crumpling, one's inner world is growing ever more secure. For John, during this period, the type of ease that was felt during the time of proficiency dissolves into a raging desolation. However, at the deepest level of one's person, a new kind of security is dimly felt.

For John, this raging dryness can last for either a long or a short time. Perhaps, too, one dies during it. However, if persevered in (and, for John, nobody turns back once he or she enters this final stage) the dryness eventually gives way to a calm, a deep peacefulness and tranquillity, which brings with it the return of passion, an overwhelming sense of the goodness of all things and of their beauty in God, a deep empathic connection with all of reality, and (for some, at least) intermittent ecstasies. This is 'Easter Sunday'. At this stage, the resurrection has taken place (save one has not yet physically died).

These, for John of the Cross, are the six stages of paschal transformation. They constitute a paradigm for how a grain of wheat is supposed to fall into the ground and die to come to new life. The dynamics inherent within this paradigm, as we shall see shortly, apply in the same way to the transformation of one's prayer life, love life and one's life of service within the community.

Before, however, illustrating this through examples, it might be profitable, in the name of pedagogy, to outline these stages more succinctly in a brief chart:

2. A chart of the six stages

(i) *Indifference... 'Pre-conversion'*
Characteristics:
- Lack of focus
- Unchannelled eros
- Gratification as the principle of motivation
- Unhealthy indifference

(ii)*Conversion... 'Falling in love'*
Characteristics:
- Focus of eros/often to point of obsession
- Change in the pleasure principle as the principle
  of motivation
- Loss of indifference

(iii) *First fervour... 'Honeymoon'*
Characteristics:
- High levels of feeling and passion/inflamed by love
- Desire for greatness and uniqueness
- Excessiveness in areas pertaining to the beloved
- Endless energy
- Public display
- Discursive appetite and abilities towards and about
  the beloved

(iv) *Waning of fervour... 'Death of the honeymoon'*
Characteristics:
- Disillusionment
- Loss of passion and consolation
- Boredom
- Loss of the discursive appetite and abilities towards
  and about the beloved
- Growing solicitousness about the beloved

(The three signs necessary to discern an authentic dark night of the soul from an inauthentic one, given by John in *The Dark Night of the Soul* Book 1, Chapter 2, should be used here.)

(v) *Proficiency... 'Growth of easefulness'*
   Characteristics:
- Decision for value
- Followed by two phases:
   (i) Dryness
   (ii) Growing easefulness, a sense of comfort-ableness, a sense of being at home, some intermittent aridities, but habitual ease.

(vi) *The final phase of growth towards transformation*
   Characteristics:
- Radical decision to live by faith alone
- Followed by a raging desolation, but with a sense of security at one's deepest level
- Eventual return to calm... which brings with it
   - the return of passion
   - an overwhelming sense of the goodness and beauty wof all things
   - a deep empathic connection with all things
   - intermittent ecstasies

3. An illustration of these stages as they apply to transformation in love, prayer and a life of service

(i) *An illustration of the transformation of love*

Since love is what a primary is everything, even in prayer and service, let us begin with an example of its transformation according to this paradigm.

Imagine a young man named Joe. He is 24 years of age, just graduated from university, and, in terms of his love life, he is in stage one, pre-conversion. He has a lot of fiery eros inside him, but he lacks focus and commitment. He is unhealthily indifferent, a state he euphemistically calls 'hanging loose'. He loves women but is not committed to any one woman. He uses women in that, in his relationships with them, he is guided by the gratification principle, that is, he is interested only to the extent that there is something in it for him. Moreover, at this stage he even feels quite moral and good about himself vis-a-vis his relationships with women. His promiscuity is, for him, not a moral issue.

One night he goes to a party and there he meets a woman named Mary. As Iris Murdoch once said, "reality can change in 15 seconds!" He falls in love. This is the moment of conversion. Immediately his indifference dies. His eros focuses most sharply. He is no longer in love with women... he is now in love with Mary and no longer wants his freedom to play the field. Promiscuity no longer interests him. Commitment to Mary does. Concomitant with this, there is a change in his motivation. He, who up until now had thought only of his own pleasure, now becomes (at least in relationship to Mary) quite generous and able to renounce many of his own wants and pleasures for her sake.

Mary also falls in love with him and soon they marry. For the first months after their marriage they are in "first fervour". He feels for her a passion and an emotional bond that relativises anything he has ever felt in relationship to anyone else. He fantasises that their marriage will be a one-in-a-million, the most unique and deepest love two people have ever shared. The love energises him and he is prone to excess in it. Also, at this stage, it is important to him to display in public that he loves Mary. They hold hands in public and, through that and other gestures, continually let the outside world

46

know that they are in love. Very importantly, during this time, he has both the appetite for and the ability to talk with Mary quite easily and quite endlessly... and when he is not talking to her he is very prone to be talking about her. He is infatuated and obsessed with her in a way that makes the indifferent Joe of just mere months ago seem an entirely different person. Naively he feels that their love will continue like this forever.

But it does not. Like all honeymoons, eventually the emotional magic is over. Imperceptibly (though in some cases this can also happen quite dramatically) the fervour lessens and, at a point, he becomes disillusioned with Mary. The disillusionment is not because he no longer sees her as a good person, but more because he begins to see her as 'just a person'. Disillusionment means the breaking of illusion and the coming to reality. After living with Mary for a time, he comes to the realisation that, despite her goodness and beauty, she is just a person, one woman... and not all of femininity and humanity incarnate. Up to this point, he had his own version of Augustine's prayer: "You have made my heart lonely, Lord, and it was lonely until it rested in Mary!" In his illusion of her, she was god/dess, femininity and humanity all in one. She was heaven. Now he is still lonely, despite Mary. Moreover, beyond this disappointment, he recognises for the first time really Mary's faults and blemishes. Thus, his disappointment, in the end, is both in that she is 'just a person' and that she is not a perfect person.

That double disappointment, that Mary is just a person and that Mary, like all of us, is also partially a dysfunctional and blemished person, brings along with it something he has never before experienced in relationship to Mary: boredom. He, at this point, begins too to lose some of the extraordinary passion and emotional feelings he had for Mary. Upsetting for him too (and perhaps even more so for Mary!) is the fact that he no longer has the same ready inclination to talk with Mary. He finds himself often without a lot to say to her, despite her pleas and his memory of seemingly better times.

However, even as the feelings of the honeymoon are dying, paradoxically, Joe is beginning, in the real sense, to be more genuinely caring for and solicitous about Mary. The joyous emotions of the honeymoon are mostly over but, despite that, he is now more deeply bonded to Mary than he was when they were on the honeymoon.

What has happened here? Why did the honeymoon die? Why do all honeymoons have to die? Is God a masochist who does not like us to have pleasure for too long?

For John of the Cross, what happens when honeymoons die (providing they die for the right reason and not because of infidelity or some kind of physical or emotional disease) is that "God takes away the passionate feelings to bring us more face-to-face with the person who is behind those feelings." Joe's honeymoon with Mary had to die because, until now, he has not been in love with Mary. Rather he has been in love with the experience... he has been in love with being in love, in love with how this made him feel, in love with femininity, in love with the goddess archetype in Mary; in short, he has been in love with many things, but not in love with Mary! Now, with the honeymoon feelings gone, after they have first served to bond him so deeply with Mary, he is left, finally, looking at Mary, at a real person. He must now decide whether or not he actually loves Mary beyond the honeymoon he has had with her.

This stage of transformation, John calls the passive night of the senses. It is a very crucial and pivotal stage within relationships. Joe can now turn back. He can leave Mary and find someone else to fall in love with and have another honeymoon. Or... he can move to the next stage and become a 'proficient' in love.

Joe does this. He makes a decision for Mary. He decides that, despite the disillusionment, he will continue in the marriage and continue to work with her in building a relationship together. His decision is based upon two things: the bond that has during the period of fervour grown up between them, and his sense of values. He senses that to continue his marriage is the right thing, the higher thing to do. He continues in the marriage.

Initially, he experiences a certain dryness in the relationship. He comes home to Mary, even though sometimes it would be more interesting for him to go elsewhere. He still struggles in the area of discursive communication with her. They both see their honeymoon stage as a certain past golden age in their relationship. Occasionally, though unsuccessfully, they try to have a second honeymoon within which to re-capture the old emotional magic.

Eventually, the dryness becomes ease. Joe still misses the magic of the honeymoon, but what he now experiences with Mary is a deepening sense of being at home. The idea and the feeling of being at home somehow melt in with his idea of Mary, his wife. There is still, intermittently, a feeling of restlessness and boredom but, habitually, there is the sense of being comfortable, easeful, at home with Mary.

Perhaps he and Mary live out their days in this proficient state. One dies or they both die. Their children and their friends sense that theirs has been a very good marriage.

Perhaps, however, given time, at some point they, together, make a most radical option. Perhaps, after years of praying together, with their children long since grown and self-sufficient, they decide, like Abraham who was asked by God to set out without knowing where he was going, to let the written word of God guide them beyond where they would go if they continued to guide themselves by practical wisdom alone. They decide, in response to the Beatitudes, to do something radical; for example, to open their home to street people, to become beggars in the style of Hindu *Sannyasins*, to live together in a religious community, or even to retire to separate monasteries.

Initially, after making this decision they feel in their relationship a new and a raging dryness. The secure sense of 'being at home', which characterised their last years together, breaks down and, with it, all their securities about each other also seemingly break down. A painful period of emotional and intellectual confusion and insecurity follows... even as neither turns back on this new radical road they have taken.

They live through this dryness, the most bitter either has ever experienced. Imperceptibly it changes and one day instead of the dryness and insecurity between them they begin to feel again a passion stronger than they felt all those years ago when they first fell in love. Moreover, along with these deep and quasi-ecstatic feelings they have for each other, they begin to feel that same kind of feelings about the world and all other people as well. They are constantly overwhelmed by the goodness and beauty not just of each other but of the whole world and everyone in it.

The emotional magic of their first honeymoon pales in comparison to this new way in which they are now inflamed by love.

Their love has now resurrected. It has fallen into the ground, died, come through 'Good Friday', and is now the kind of love that will last and grow forever. There will be no death of this second honeymoon. There will only be passion, joy and ecstatic union of life forever. When John of the Cross speaks of going through the dark night of the soul, it is this process he is describing.

(ii)*An illustration of the transformation of prayer*

Just as love must go through a certain dark night of the soul in order to come to full maturity, so too must prayer. The stages of transformation and the dynamics inherent in the movement from stage to stage are identical. So too are the characteristics of each stage.

Let us imagine a young woman named Mary. She is 24 years of age, just graduated from university, and, in terms of her prayer life, is at stage one, 'pre-conversion'. She does not have much interest in prayer, has no habit of prayer and, most times, simply does not pray. In her prayer life, and in her religious life in general, she lacks focus and is unhealthily indifferent. She is guided by the gratification principle in that she prays and/or attends religious services when in some way there is something in it for her.

One evening, out of boredom and to tag along with friends, she goes to a Charismatic prayer meeting. As Iris Murdoch says... 'reality can change in 15 seconds!" She has a religious experience and is overcome with both the desire to pray and the facility for it. She is baptised in the Spirit and, among other things, begins to speak in tongues. She has fallen in love, been 'converted'.

Immediately, not unlike the person who has fallen in love with another person, she enters 'first fervour'. She has, in prayer, intense emotional feelings and is spontaneously moved to tears, to deep joy, to deep feelings of empathy for the world, and to an intense desire to serve God completely to the point of giving up her life. With that come fantasies of uniqueness and greatness. Mary believes that she can be a great saint, a mystic even. In her daydreams she will pray and serve God like very few others ever have. Like the young lover, she is full of endless energy and is prone to excess in her prayer life. She goes to prayer meetings nearly every evening and

51

stays there too long. It is also important for her, during this time, to publicly display her new love, to let the world know that she has found Christ. Her car is covered with stickers reading "I have found Christ', 'Christ Saves', 'God loves you', and so on. Around her neck she wears a cross and on her lapel is pinned a dove. A pagan world is invited constantly to see that she has found Christ. At this time, too, she has both the appetite for and the ability for discursive prayer. She can pray easily and endlessly. When she is not praying she is, much to the chagrin of her friends, talking about praying! And, like the young lover, she naively believes that things will carry on like this forever.

But they do not. Imperceptibly, or perhaps dramatically, things change. There comes a day when the fervour is gone. Her honeymoon in prayer is over. She enters the passive night of the senses, the 'waning of fervour'. Like the lover, she begins to experience disillusionment, the loss of consolation, boredom, and the loss of both the appetite and capacity for discursive prayer. She becomes disillusioned with her prayer life and, oftentimes, with her prayer group as well. Her bible, within which during her time of fervour she underlined in different bright colours nearly every line because it was so meaningful, now bores her. She finds herself unable to pray as she did before and feels no passion or emotion in her prayer.

However, if these symptoms are not the result of infidelity or emotional or physical illness, then, even as her fervour is waning, she will experience, at a level beyond her emotions and even her intellect, a desire for prayer and a solicitousness about God and the things of religion. She will no longer have the magical emotional feelings about prayer she once had, nor will she have the ability to pray discursively as she used to. But she will want to pray... even as she is unsure as to what that now means.

Again, it is useful to insert a reflection at this point. Why did her honeymoon in prayer die?

Like the lover, her honeymoon had to die because, during her period of fervour, she was not so much interested in God as she was in the experience of praying and how that made her feel. For John, in the passive night of the senses, God dries up the experience so as to give the person a chance to meet more face-to-face the person behind the experience. God dried up her experience of prayer so as to give her the opportunity, after the honeymoon had first done its work of bonding her to God more deeply, of being interested in God and not just in the experience of praying.

And Mary is now interested in God. Although she is somewhat confused and disappointed about the death of her fervour, she now decides that she will pray not because it feels good but because she is now interested in God. She makes a decision for prayer and, with that, enters 'proficiency'.

Initially she experiences mostly dryness in her prayer. Unable to pray as she formerly did, discursively, she spends her prayer time just sitting quietly. Slowly the dryness of this gives way to a certain comfortableness in it. Her prayer time is not an exciting time but it is a good time, an easeful time, a time when she feels very centred, at home, and somehow in God's presence. She still has intermittent aridities in her prayer but mostly she experiences ease and a sense of comfort and of being at home.

This can continue for a short time or a long time. Perhaps she dies during the months or years of 'proficiency'. If she does die, she will die, in John of the Cross' eyes, quite advanced, but not fully transformed, in the spiritual life.

However, in this case she does not die during this stage and, after some time in it, she senses inchoately that God is now asking something more radical of her.

Like Abraham, she senses that God is now calling her to set out "without knowing where she is going".

Her prayer life has, in effect, now become her whole life. She realises that, until now, she has been partially rationalising and not giving herself over fully to the demands of the Sermon on the Mount. She makes the decision that from now on she will no longer use her practical vision and the 'friendly counsel' of her family and friends to smooth away the sharp edges of the demands of the Sermon on the Mount. She decides to live her life rather 'fundamentalistically' in the light of those demands.

What this means practically can vary from case to case. Perhaps she runs off and joins Mother Theresa, or becomes a Trappistine nun, or becomes a Christian *Sannyasin*, or she gives almost all her money and possessions away and lives most austerely. Like the couple, Joe and Mary, we spoke of earlier, entry into the dark night of the spirit can take many practical forms. Whatever its specific form, it takes place when, after a sufficient time of preparation, a person uses the written word of God to actually guide him or her in life, beyond the dictates of common sense, practical wisdom and the measured advice of those biblical commentators and spiritual directors who are unfamiliar with this final phase of paschal transformation.

Mary makes this radical leap of faith. Her family and friends are very upset with her. They worry about her. But this is not her greatest pain and insecurity. Rather, almost immediately upon making this decision, she herself is thrown into raging desolation. She feels disconsolate and feels that God has let her down. At times she even has severe faith doubts and begins to wonder whether God in fact exists. The habitual ease and sense of being at home, which she had just recently felt in prayer, now too disappears. She feels lost... beyond any hope that anyone can offer her. That is why she is not interested in the advice of concerned family and friends who suggest that what she should do to regain her 'old self' is to go back on her radical decision and live a 'normal' life, like everyone else. At this stage, Mary knows that 'a normal life' is not her hope. Nothing turns her back. She stays with the pain and confusion, knowing that, as the author of Lamentations says, there are times when one can only put one's mouth in the dust and wait!

She waits and one day it is better. One day (and John says we cannot predict whether it will take a long time or a short time for that day to arrive) there is in Mary not dryness but a passionate fervour. A fervour deeper than what she felt all those years ago at that prayer meeting where she had her religious conversion. Passionate fervour now begins to stir habitually inside of her. The fervour is so intense that, intermittently, it is ecstatic. In it, she experiences an overwhelming sense of the reality and graciousness of God, as well as a concomitant sense of the overwhelming goodness and beauty of all of creation. She has trouble containing her sense of this goodness and finds herself, occasionally, 'standing outside of herself', that is, in *ek stasis*.

Mary's prayer life has now undergone the dark night of the soul. The seed which was there at her initial conversion has fallen into the ground and died and brought forth new and eternal life. The feelings she now feels will never die. She has moved beyond being interested in herself and in the experience of prayer to being interested in God. Good Friday is over. She is now living Easter Sunday.

(iii) *An illustration of the transformation of service*

The dynamics which mark the transformation of love and prayer are parallelled in the transformation of our service within community.

55

Let me illustrate this with a real-life example (stylised a bit to protect the person whose story it is).

A few years ago, I knew a young man who, upon graduating from university, had very little, if any, interest in social justice and the poor. He was interested in his own career advancement, his own social circle, and in sex, travel and the enjoyment of his youth.

As a graduation gift, his parents gave him several thousand dollars which he was using to go on a six-month tour with some friends of his. Their tour was, eventually, to take them to South America where their chief interest was not the poor but the beaches and the good life.

However, as C.S. Lewis once said, conversion can be most surprising. While in South America he broke his tour with his friends for one week to visit with a Canadian missionary whose mother was a neighbour of his family back home. He met the poor and, like the person who falls in love or the person who has a religious experience at a prayer meeting, his life radically changed in 15 seconds. He saw the poor and something inside of him irrevocably moved. In that moment he lost his unhealthy indifference and he moved beyond the pleasure principle as his simple motivation for acting. In that moment he 'converted'.

Like the young man in love and like the woman at the prayer meeting, with that conversion came 'first fervour'. He broke with his friends and returned home. Once there, rather than pick up what would have been his career, teaching, he instead began to work at the local food bank, lived on virtually nothing and got involved with numerous groups who are active in social justice activities.

And he had a honeymoon of fervour. As he worked with and for the poor, he was inflamed with feelings about them. He had too, like the lover and the religious neophyte, fantasies of uniqueness and greatness. In his daydreams, he was the world's greatest social worker. Like his counterparts in love and prayer, he had too, at this stage, endless energy and was prone to excess. He worked endless hours for the poor and still spent many of his evenings at meetings discussing projects, protests and political programmes. And, like the young lover and the religious novice, it was important to him at this time to make public display of his commitment. His car too was covered with stickers: 'Boycott Shell', 'Resist the USA in Central America', 'God is a woman... Listen to her!', and so on. His designer clothes hung unworn in his closet while he wore only certain khakis and denims. At this time, parallel to what happens to those who have had a recent conversion in love or prayer, he had both the appetite and ability for certain discursiveness. In his case, this took the form of an endless ability to talk to the poor and an equal ability to talk about them – when he was not talking to them. At this time, too, he was under the naive impression that he would feel like that forever.

He did not. There came a day, a few years later, when the fervour was gone, the honeymoon over. Perfectly parallel to what happens when the first fervour of love and prayer die, he began to feel, in his relationship to the poor, disillusion, a loss of passion, boredom, and the loss of his former discursive powers towards and for them. Now his words seem, to him, to be empty and he draws little consolation in talking to them or in talking to others about them. He prefers to say a lot less.

That is the stage my friend is in at present. However since, in his case, his commitment to the poor had been genuine, he is still deeply committed to the poor and genuinely solicitous for them, even in his lack of felt consolation in serving them.

Again, an important question needs to be raised here: Why did his fervour die? Why did God dry up the experience?

Like the case of the lover and the woman in prayer, God took away all natural consolation in the experience so that this young man might be brought more face-to-face with what is behind the experience, the poor themselves. Until that stage, the waning of fervour (the passive night of the senses), he had not been in love with the poor but in love with the experience of serving the poor and in love with how that made him feel.

I judge my friend to be, right now, in the stage of 'proficiency'. He is serving the poor, just as he did while in fervour. His decision to continue to serve was based not upon the naive hope that, some day, he would again experience pleasure in serving the poor but upon a real bond he has built up with the poor during his years of commitment to them. He serves them now because they are, in a real sense, his family. He loves them, not with passion of first fervour but with the type of concern that one has for a family member. There is considerable emotional dryness in him but, as time passes, there is too a growing sense of ease, comfortableness and at-homeness with the poor.

I do not know how his story will end. Perhaps he will serve the poor in this way until he dies. If he does, he will die essentially unselfish, living out in a good, though imperfect, fashion, Christ's preferential option for the poor. Perhaps however, given a long life and much grace, he will, at some point, make a yet more radical option for the poor and, through that, enter into the final stage of transformation.

Like his counterpart in love and prayer, he would enter this final stage if, on the basis of the written word of Scripture, he would make a choice to serve the poor in a way that goes beyond what practical wisdom and a qualified commitment would demand. What specific form that might take can vary; for example, perhaps he will go to a poor country and work there in the style of Mother Teresa perhaps he will live and work in a hospice for cancer or aids victims, or perhaps he will join L'Arche and spend the rest of his life simply living with handicapped adults.

Whatever he does, initially, that choice will bring him some raging desolation and much disorientation. Whatever moral securities he might have built up during his previous years of service with and to the poor will totally break. He will spend some time, either a long time or a short time, totally unable to reassure himself or to give himself any practical hope. The only reassurance and hope he will have will come to him through raw faith in the Word of God and the Eucharist. He will be disconsolate, but he will not turn back.

Eventually, a new day will dawn and he will awake one day to find that his passion has returned. He will be inflamed with a love for the poor that dwarfs anything he felt all those years ago when he first converted. With that will come an overwhelming sense of the goodness and beauty, not just of the poor but of all of creation. He will live in a state of habitual joy and will, at moments, be unable to contain the sense of how good and beautiful it all is. He will have intermittent ecstasies and he will be inflamed with a joy "that no one will ever take away from him".

SOME CONCLUDING NOTES

These examples illustrate the process of transformation that John of the Cross calls the dark night of the soul. We see, too, through these examples, that, although John outlined the stages of this transformation only by articulating the dynamic movement inherent within prayer, these dynamics have a perfect parallel within love and service.

Human life and every dimension within it must, if it is to come to eternal life, fall into the ground and die in order to rise again. Christ illustrated this in his person through the paschal mystery in his journey through Good Friday to Easter Sunday. What John of the Cross outlines, both descriptively and prescriptively, in his metaphor of the dark night of the soul is how this passage takes place concretely within our lives (beyond its more radical form in our actual physical death).

The dark night of the soul is, then, a metaphor for paschal transformation. For purposes of clarity and simplicity, this essay has broken it into six clear stages, with the hope that the attempt at clarity would not do too much violence to the complexity and subtlety of John's position, and that it would serve, so to speak, as a work of 'translation' in making this most valuable concept of John of the Cross more accessible to a larger number of people.

Kevin G. Culligan

John of the Cross and human relationships: An essay in sexuality and spirituality

This is a theme that is neglected by the Church; i.e, seeing the compatibility between sexuality and spirituality. We believe that John has some very important insights and guidelines.

Embodied spirits that we are, human relationships always involve sexuality. For this reason, I subtitle my talk: *An essay in sexuality and spirituality.* Today I want to concentrate on St John of the Cross and human sexuality. Writers like Michael Dodd, Richard Hardy and the Spanish authors of the new pictorial biography of St John of the Cross honouring the fourth centenary of his death have convincingly demonstrated the positive role human friendship played in John's life.[1] However, the place of sexuality in his life and writings still awaits treatment. Today I want to discuss this topic with you, hoping thereby to direct public attention to this important dimension of human life and trusting that further studies will follow in the years ahead.

Sexuality and spirituality is an important topic for several reasons. First, we live as human beings in a postmodern age, the information era, in which we are developing increasingly sophisticated means of communications which, paradoxically, tend to further isolate us from one another. Learning to live intimately with one another – physically, emotionally, spiritually – is becoming increasingly necessary for human survival.

Secondly, the Second Vatican Council, in stating that all Christians are called to holiness, has dramatically revolutionised our ideas of Christian spirituality. If the call to be holy comes primarily from Baptism and Confirmation, not from sacred orders and religious profession, then our earlier models of holiness, most of which have been developed by celibate clergy and religious, must be widened to include the experience of laity, married and non-married, particularly the daily experience of sexuality. For example: sexual intercourse is essential to the sacrament of matrimony; therefore, contemporary models of Christian spirituality must integrate sense and spirit rather than place them in opposition to each other as celibate models of holiness tend to do.

More importantly, our failure to integrate sexuality into Christian spirituality is causing great pain among all God's people, at least in the country I come from, but I suspect in your country as well. We see married couples whose relationship is strained because one or both parties feel ashamed of their bodies, consider love-making inferior to prayer and asceticism, or misapply John of the Cross's teaching on mortification of sensory appetites to their sexual relations. For clergy and religious, the Church is now paying millions upon millions of dollars to settle sexual abuse cases, mostly involving paedophilia. Within the last year, two North American Archbishops have resigned their Sees because of sex related scandals. And, finally, single Catholics wonder realistically whether it is possible to be chaste in a culture that glorifies sex and ridicules chastity as inhuman.

To address these issues, the American bishops have for over a decade recognised the need for education in human sexuality. In November 1990, they approved a document entitled *Human Sexuality: A Catholic Perspective for Education and Life-long Learning*. In it, they call the entire Catholic people to sex education. They write:

One's growth in understanding human sexuality does not end with puberty or marriage or some subsequent threshold in life. The Catholic Church teaches that human life is to be valued and safeguarded from the moment of conception. The need to relate sexual feelings with the Christian call to love and be loved is a life-long task for each of us. Education in sexuality is a continual process, an invitation for each of us to grow and develop as morally mature sexual beings, whatever our age or calling in life. We encourage ongoing formation in human sexuality not only for children and adolescents but also for all people, particularly during major transitions in life (e.g., puberty, moving away from home, engagement/marriage, parenthood, middle age, retirement, divorce or widowhood, ordination, religious vows, ageing, serious illness).

It behoves all of us [the bishops conclude their introductory chapter] to approach the mystery of incarnation and our sexuality with a degree of humility.

We are aware of the depth and complexity of the topic. This document is offered as our contribution to the ongoing discussion about what it means to be mature sexual persons – physically, psychologically, socially and spiritually whole.[2]

"The need to relate sexual feelings with the Christian call to love and be loved is a life-long task for each of us" and "to be mature sexual persons – physically, psychologically, socially and spiritually whole": in these two phrases the bishops set out the parameters for a contemporary model of holiness, one which attempts to integrate every aspect of human life into our never-ending effort to give and receive love. The question I want to consider with you today is this: can John of the Cross contribute anything to such a holistic approach to spirituality in which intimate human relationships are as essential as daily fidelity to God's merciful love?

A few definitions

Before attempting to answer that question, let me give a few definitions. By spirituality, I mean that dimension of human life which is oriented to the transcendent, however defined, and seeks human fulfilment beyond satisfaction of the senses. In this broad sense, spirituality is a quest common to the entire human family, regardless of racial origin or religious preference. Most specifically, Christian spirituality is "the living out in experience, throughout the whole course of our lives, of the death-resurrection of Christ that we have been caught up into by Baptism."[3]

By sexuality, I mean "a relational power, not merely a capacity for performing specific acts":

Sexuality refers to a fundamental component of personality in and through which we, as male and female, experience our relatedness to self, others, the world and even God.

Ultimately, sexuality is God's gift: "In its fullest and richest sense, the gift of sexuality is both the physical and psychological grounding for the human person's capacity to love... It is a gift shared by all persons, regardless of their state in life."

A related, but distinct, reality is sex, by which I mean, first of all, "the biological aspects of being male or female (i.e., a synonym for one's gender)". This is what I say of myself when I respond to the question M or F on application forms. Sex also refers to "the expressions of sexuality, which have physical, emotional and spiritual dimensions, particularly genital actions resulting in sexual intercourse and/or orgasm". In this sense, we speak of "having sex".[4]

These definitions recognise that sexuality implies far more than sex. They also imply that the challenge of integrating sexuality and spirituality is not met simply by applying certain moral criteria to specific sexual acts; rather, it is the integration of the person I am as centred in this body (sexuality) and with the longing I experience deep within me, that never goes away, for union with God (spirituality).

John of the Cross

At first glance, it appears that John of the Cross has little to offer this integration process. His early biographers pictured him as a stern ascetic whose longing for 'God Alone" made him avoid intimate human relationships and subdue his body with unremitting penance. Indeed, his writings seem to present a world-denying spirituality which opposes sense and spirit and depreciates human interaction.

For example, John writes in *The Ascent of Mount Carmel*: All the delights and satisfactions of the will in the things of the world in contrast to all the delight that is God is intense suffering, torment and bitterness. Persons who link their hearts to these delights, then, deserve in God's eyes intense suffering, torment and bitterness. They will be incapable of attaining the delights of the embrace of union with God, since they merit suffering and bitterness (A 1,4,7).

Later, in the same book, he states: "The perfect spirit pays no attention to the senses; it neither receives anything through them, nor uses them principally, nor judges them to be requisite in its relationship with God, as it did before its spiritual growth" (A 2,17,6).

And, to cite a final example, John writes: "Since nothing equals God, a person who loves and is attached to something other than God, or together with God, offends God exceedingly" (A 1,5,5; cf A 1,11,5).

These statements, I think you will agree, may be fine for the sixteenth-century Spanish Carmelite friars and nuns for whom they were written; but, they hardly inspire confidence that John has much to contribute to a contemporary conjugal or familial spirituality.

A closer look at John's life, however, reveals a different picture. From the very beginning of his existence on earth, he was a 'child of love'. He was born of parent who married because they loved each other, not because their families arranged their union according to the current custom of Spanish society. For this decision, John's father, Gonzalo de Yepez, was disowned by his family. He and his wife, Catalina Alvarez, were forced to earn their living as poor weavers and to bear their three sons in poverty.

Shortly after John's birth, his father Gonzalo died. His mother, Catalina, was now reduced to the ranks of the itinerant poor, moving wherever necessary to provide for her family. Nevertheless, there was always room in their home for those poorer than themselves. Records show that Catalina accepted abandoned babies into her home, cared for them, arranged for their Baptism, and found permanent homes for them.

From his mother and older brother, Francisco, John learned lessons of love for the poor and sick which he practised throughout his life. After his entry into the Carmelites, he maintained deep bonds of affection for his mother and Francisco and his family. In later years, he arranged for them to live in the monastery with him and help with the community's domestic and maintenance needs. He considered his older brother, Francisco, "the treasure I love most in the whole world".[5]

As a Carmelite, John was also a good brother to his Carmelite brothers and sisters. He participated fully in the active life of the community and valued his close companionship to Fray Juan de Santa Ana and Fray Juan Evangelista. His letters reveal that he was a trusted and faithful friend to his Carmelites sisters, both communities and individuals. For the last thirteen years of his life, he was particularly close to Madre Ana de Jesús Lobera, to whom he dedicated his commentary on *The Spiritual Canticle*.

As a spiritual director, John also extended himself beyond the walls of Carmel to men and women on what might best be called a ministry of love. He dedicated, *The Living Flame of Love*, both poem and commentary, to Doña Ana de Mercado y Peñalosa, a widow, benefactress, directee, and a woman to whom he could open himself freely in his letters. (Letters of 19 August and 21 September, 1591 to Doña Ana de Mercado y Peñalosa from La Penuela.) The depth of intimacy he established with his spiritual daughters may perhaps be best seen in two letters to Juana de Pedraza (c. 1557-c. 1673), a woman in her early thirties.

John was Juana'a spiritual director when he was stationed in Granada from 1582 to 1588. Following his transfer to Segovia in 1586, he continued to guide her by letter. Responding to her complaints of spiritual dryness, John wrote to Juana on 28 January 1589 from Segovia:

Jesus be in your soul.

A few days ago I wrote to you through Padre Fray Juan in answer to your last letter, which, as was your hope, I prized... And I have felt your grief, afflictions and loneliness. These, in silence, ever tell me so much that the pen cannot declare it.

After encouraging patience in her trials, John concludes: "Commend me to God, and, when you can, give your letters to Fray Juan (Evangelista) or to the nuns more often — and it would be better if they (your letters) were not so short" (letter to Juana de Pedraza of 28 January 1589, from Segovia).

Months passed and apparently Juana's desolation did not lift. She wrote again to John in Segovia, explaining her condition and, it appears, reprimanding him for forgetting her, apparently because he had not written. He responds in a letter written 12 October 1589, from Segovia.

Jesus be in your soul and thanks to him that he has enabled me not to forget the poor, as you say, or be idle, as you say. For it greatly vexes me to think you believe what you say; this would be very bad after so many kindnesses on your part when I least deserved them. That's all I need now is to forget you! Look, how could this be in the case of one who is in my soul as you are? (letter to Juana de Pedraza, 12 October 1589, from Segovia).

Some eight to ten years before his letter to Juana, when John was composing *The Ascent of Mount Carmel*, he stated in Book One:

All objects living in the soul – whether they may be many or few, large or small – must die in order that the soul enter divine union, and it must bear or desire for them but remain detached as though they were non-existent to it, and it to them (A 1,11,8).

Our brief review of John's own life suggests that his family, his fellow friars and nuns, and the laity he served in ministry were hardly non-existent to him, nor he to them, rather in contrast to what he wrote in the *Ascent*, he appears to have carried them deep within his own heart.

John's use of erotic imagery

John's comfort with human intimacy may be seen even more clearly by examining his use of erotic imagery to describe the intimate union between the human person and God. These images of human sexual love are found principally in *The Spiritual Canticle* and *The Living Flame of Love*, treatises written during the last seven years of his life after he completed *The Ascent of Mount Carmel* and *The Dark Night*, both of them written for women.

A man and woman, for example, look deeply into each others eyes and communicate their mutual love without words. John uses this 'look of love' in his poem, *The Spiritual Canticle*, as he describes the human person's longing for Jesus Christ.

4. O woods and thickets
   Planted by the hand of my beloved!
   O green meadow,
   Coated, bright, with flowers,
   Tell me, has he passed by you?

5. Pouring out a thousand graces,
   He passed these groves in haste;
   And having looked at them,
   With his image alone,
   Clothed them in beauty.

10. Extinguish these miseries,
    Since no one else can stamp them out;
    And may my eyes behold you,
    Because you are their light
    And I would open them to you alone.

11. Reveal your presence,
    And may the vision of your beauty be my death;
    For the sickness of love
    is not cured
    Except by your very presence and image.

12. O spring like crystal!
    If only, on your silvered over-face,
    you would suddenly form the eyes I have
    desired
    Which I bear sketched deep within my heart.
13. Withdraw them, Beloved,
    I am taking flight!

Commenting on these verses, John writes:-

"And may my eyes behold you", that is: May I see
you face to face with the eyes of my soul, "because
you are their light". Regardless of the fact that God is
the supernatural light of the soul's eyes, and that
without this light she is enveloped in darkness, she
affectionately calls (God) here the light of her eyes,
just as a man might call the one he loves the light of
his eyes in order to show his affection.

"And I would open them to you alone": with this
line the soul desires to oblige the bridegroom to reveal this light of her eyes not only because she lives
in darkness in that her eyes have no other light, but
also because she wants to keep her eyes for him alone
(C 10,7-9).

Lovers, also, use fragrances to attract each other, as
today's commercials for perfume, cologne and after-
shave lotion frequently remind us. John uses this image
to describe the mutual attraction that God and the human person have for one another. In the *Living Flame of
Love*, he writes:

... if a person is seeking God, God (the Beloved) is
seeking the person much more. And if a person di-
rects to God its loving desires, which are as fragrant
(to God) as the pillar of smoke rising from the aro-
matic spices of myrrh and incense (Ct 3:5), God sends
the person the fragrance of his ointments by which

he draws it and makes it run after him (Ct 1:3), and these are God's divine inspiration and touches... The desire for himself which God grants in all his favours of unguents and fragrant anointings is a preparation for other more precious and delicate ointments, made more according to the quality of God, until the person is so delicately and purely prepared that it merits union with God and substantial transformation in all its faculties (F 3,28).

In this analogy, God is a 'seductive lover'. Our desires for God are like a fragrance drawing God toward us; but, even more powerfully, like a woman using expensive perfume to draw her man close to her, so the divine inspirations and touches of God in our soul are like powerful fragrances which God uses to draw us to himself and to prepare us for divine union.

Finally, John uses human lovemaking – the exploration of bodies, the kissing of breasts, the mutual surrender and losing of self in orgasm – to describe the mutual surrender of God and the human person. Describing the spiritual espousal, the bride in *The Spiritual Canticle* states poetically:

24. Our bed is in flower,
     Bound round with linking dens of lions,
     Hung with purple,
     Built up in peace,
     And crowned with a thousand shields of gold.
26. In the inner wine cellar
     I drank of my beloved, and, when I went abroad
     Through all this valley
     I no longer knew anything,
     And lost the herd which I was following.
27. There he gave me his breast;
     There he taught me a sweet and living
     knowledge;

And I gave myself to him,
Keeping nothing back;
There I promised to be his bride.
28. Now I occupy my soul
And all my energy in his service;
I no longer tend the herd,
Nor have I any other work
Now that my every act is love.
29. If, then, I am no longer
Seen or found on the common,
You will say that I am lost;
That, stricken by love,
I lost myself, and was found.

Commenting on the stanza beginning "There he gave me his breast", John writes:

In this stanza the bride tells of the mutual surrender made in this spiritual espousal between the person and God, saying that in that interior wine cellar of love they were joined by the communication he made of himself to her, by freely offering her the breast of his love, in which he taught her wisdom and secrets, and by the complete surrender she made of herself to him keeping nothing back for herself or for any other, promising to be his forever. The verse follows: 'There he gave me his breast.' Giving one's breast to another signifies the giving of love and friendship to another and the revealing of secrets to him as to a friend. When the person says that there he gave her his breast, she means that he communicated his love and secrets to her there. God grants this communication to the soul in this state (C 27,3-4).

In his commentary on the verse "I lost myself, and was found", John explains:

The person affirms here that she lost herself. She achieved this in two ways: she became lost to herself by paying no attention to herself in anything, by concentrating on her beloved and surrendering herself to him freely and disinterestedly, with no desire to gain anything for herself; secondly, she became lost to all creatures, paying no heed to all her own affairs, but only to those of her beloved. And this is to lose herself purposely, which is to desire to be found.

He who walks in the love of God seeks neither his own gain nor his reward, but only to lose all things and himself for God; and this loss he judges to be his gain. And thus it is as St Paul asserts: *"Mori lucrum"* (Phil 1:21), that is, my death for Christ is the spiritual gain of all things and of myself. And consequently the soul declares: I was found. He who does not know how to lose himself does not find himself but rather loses himself, as Our Lord teaches in the Gospel: "He who desires to gain his soul shall lose it, and he who loses it for my sake will gain it" (Mt 16:35) (C 29,10-11).

In these passages, John draws upon the experience of human lovemaking, not only to describe the intimate union of God and the human person but also to interpret the Gospel of Jesus. In the orgasm that climaxes human lovemaking, persons lose control of themselves in their mutual surrender to each other, only to discover themselves anew in the union their lovemaking creates. Persons whose need for control or inability to trust their lover prevents them from surrendering themselves never discover the new person they can be in union with another. He or she remains simply unchanged, clinging to the known past, unafraid of the unknown future. So too, John teaches, we shall never discover the new person Jesus calls us to be in union with him unless we are willing to surrender ourselves completely to him in total trust.

These passages from *The Spiritual Canticle* and *Living Flame of Love* suffice to illustrate how comfortably John of the Cross uses images of human love to convey something of the ultimately ineffable experience of the spiritual marriage between God and the human person. He can do so, I believe, because of his unqualified acceptance of the goodness of all human creation, made good simply because the eyes of the beloved, the Lord Jesus, behold all creation and, in that loving gaze, make all things good, just as a woman feels herself to be thoroughly good, good all over, when she sees her lover looking upon her with eyes of love (C 4-7).

Let us return now to the creation passage from Book 1 Chapter 4 of *The Ascent of Mount Carmel* which I quoted earlier. John's apparently negative judgement of creation in that chapter is softened if we notice the words 'in comparison' or 'in contrast with' in each of his statements. All creatures 'compared with' the infinite beauty and goodness of God are nothing, although in themselves they are good and beautiful because God creates and sustains them, and Jesus Christ looks upon them. And we most experience their goodness and beauty to the degree we ourselves are centred in God. By contrast, if we seek created things for themselves alone, apart from God, we discover painfully their inherent limitations. "All things betray thee", says the voice of Francis Thompson's *The Hound of Heaven*, 'who betrayest me... Lo! naught contents thee, who content'st not me." God created things, not to be sought as ends in themselves but to enrich our love affair with him. Human relationships, above all, enhance God's love for us and our love for God.[6]

A closer reading of John also reveals that, rather than separating sense and spirit, he sees them as two distinct but inextricably related areas of human life which constitute the whole person. Despite the various faculties, capacities and operations of sense and spirit, the human person is, ultimately, an integrated whole which John calls 'this whole harmonious composite' – *toda esta harmonia*, in Spanish (N 2,11,4; C 16,5). Describing the 'vehement passion of divine love' – *vehemente pasion de amor divino* – which is a fruit of the dark night of spirit, John thus refers to the human person in Book 2 of *The Dark Night*.

> One might, then, in a certain way ponder how remarkable and how strong this enkindling of love in the spirit can be. God gathers together all the strength, faculties and appetites of the soul, sensory and spiritual alike, that the energy and power of this whole harmonious composite may be employed in this love. The person consequently arrives at the true fulfilment of the first commandment which, neither disdaining anything human nor excluding it from his love, states: "You shall love your God with your whole heart and with your whole mind and with your whole soul and with all your strength" (Dt 6:5) (N 2,11,4; cf C 16,5 and 10; F 3,7).

Because the human person is a harmonious composite of sense and spirit, both are involved in our relationship with God. We need our senses to grow in faith because, as St Paul reminds us, "faith comes through hearing" (Rom 10:17; A 2,3,3). At the same time, experiences of God deep within our spirit are often manifested in our senses, in deeply-felt emotions such as joy in God's presence, fear of God's absence or sorrow in offending God. The inextricable relationship of sense and spirit means further that the ecstasy of physical orgasm is potentially as much religious experience as ecstatic moments of prayer deep in the spirit. Thus, because the whole person – sense and spirit – is involved in one's relationship with God, John easily uses images that are primarily sensual to describe human transformation in God, which is ultimately spiritual.

Finally, this transformation of the human person in God is a work of love, or better, is divine love at work in the human person. Love, whether human or divine in origin, always involves an awakening and mutual attraction, sensory pleasure, renunciation, fidelity, dryness, purification, mutual surrender, commitment and, finally, union of two persons. John expresses this fundamental mystery of human life through various images – a journey up a mountain, marriage, a fire transforming a log into itself. But, in the end, love is love, whether divine or human, and the one is best understood by reference to the other. If John uses blissful examples from human love to teach us about divine love, he also reminds us, as he wrote to a Carmelite nun shortly before he died, that God allows suffering in our interpersonal relationships so that we might learn to love one another "by means of the very love God bears towards us" (letter to a Discalced Carmelite nun in Segovia, from Ubeda, October-November 1591). In a tone unmistakably autobiographical, John writes in *The Living Flame of Love* that, for one whose consciousness has been transformed in God, it seems "that the entire universe is a sea of love in which it is engulfed, for, conscious of the living point or centre of love within itself, it is unable to catch sight of the boundaries of this love" (F 2,10).

Thus, the best interpreters of any single passage of John's writings – especially those which appear to devalue creation, to oppose sense and spirit, or to distrust human relationships – are the story of his whole life and all his writings. Indeed, viewed with this broader perspective, John becomes, I contend, a valuable resource for learning to integrate spirituality and sexuality in the pursuit of perfect love, the ideal of Christian holiness.

One can find for example, in John's Book 3, Chapters 21-26 of *The Ascent of Mount Carmel* and in Book 1 Chapter 4 of *The Dark Night*, guidelines for integrating our primary sexuality (our feelings about our body, about our self as a man or woman), our genital sexuality (behaviour, thoughts, fantasies, desires and feelings associated with genital arousal resulting in sexual intercourse and/or orgasm), and our affective sexuality (feeling close to others and ability to express this closeness in word and touch) with one's relationship with God.[7] On first reading, these chapters, which speak of our relationship to natural and sensory goods and the imperfections of lust found in beginners in the spiritual life, seem out of date, negative, and impossible to apply in today's world. A closer study, however, using the hermeneutical tools of John's entire life and writings and the present, although imperfect, state of our knowledge of sexuality from the human sciences, will, I believe, reveal guidelines for integrating our sexual experience into our relationship with God, our primary human relationship, and into Gospel living. From there, one can apply these guidelines to conjugal and family spirituality, vowed celibacy, the single life for the sake of the kingdom, persons with a homosexual orientation, and the numerous other questions related to human sexuality, both healthy and unhealthy.

A heuristic approach

We best explore this relationship between sexuality and spirituality heuristically, that is, with an attitude open to new discoveries, rather than with a mind that already has all the answers. Archbishop Rembert G. Weakland OSB, former Abbot Primate of the Benedictines and now Ordinary of the Archdiocese of Milwaukee, Wisconsin, reflected this attitude in a statement to a conference on the "Future of the American Church". He said:

> We will have to continue to be humble with regard to all sexual issues that face us in the next decades. Human science simply does not have the answers, and it is very difficult to base our moral judgements on imperfect knowledge. In such a case we have to realise the imperfection of the whole process. We have indeed much to learn.[8]

Indeed, we have much to learn. However, if we can bring our experience as sexual persons, committed in faith to following the Gospel's law of love, into dialogue with the Church's ancient wisdom about human life and the discoveries about human life from contemporary science, we will discover, I believe, a way of being with God, self and one another that fully responds to Jesus's call "to be humanly whole and spiritually holy"[9]. In this dialogue, St John of the Cross, Mystical Doctor of the Church, Teacher of Faith, can be an instructive voice. He upholds the goodness of all creation, provides a holistic view of the human person that integrates sense and spirit in the quest for union with God, and stresses the primacy of love in Christian life. Most importantly, he appreciates and celebrates, in moving poetry and enlightening commentary, human love as a powerful image for "the vehement passion of divine love" (N 2,11, title).

NOTES

1. Michael Dodd OCD, "Saint John of the Cross and Friendship", *Spiritual Life* 26 (Winter 1980), pp. 194-204; Richard Hardy, *Search for Nothing: The Life of John of the Cross*, New York: Crossroad, 1982; Federico Ruiz OCD, Jose Vicente Rodriquez OCD et al., *Dios Habla en la Noche: Vida Palabra Ambiente de San Juan de la Cruz*, Madrid: Editorial de Espiritualidad, 1990.

2. *Human Sexuality: A Catholic Perspective for Education and Life-long Learning*, Washington D.C.: United States Catholic Conference, Inc., 1990, pp. 4-6.
3. *Ibid.*, p. 17.
4. *Ibid.*, pp. 8-9.
5. Redemptus Maria Valabek, "The Saintly Brother of a Saint: The Brother of St John of the Cross – Francisco de Yepes, Carmelite Tertiary", *Carmel in the World*, 29 (1990, no. 2), 135-52.
6. Ross Collings OCD, *John of the Cross*, Collegeville, Minnesota: A Michael Glazier Book/The Liturgical Press, 1990. See especially Chapter 2, "Creation: 'By the Hand of the Beloved'", pp. 26-60.
7. Discussion of primary, genital and affective sexuality may be found in William F. Kraft, *Whole and Holy Sexuality: How to Find Human and Spiritual Integrity as a Sexual Person*, St Meinrad, Indiana: Abbey Press, 1989; and in Patricia H. Livingston, *Made for Union, Meant for Love: Claiming our Sexuality*, Notre Dame, Indiana: Ave Maria Press/Modern Cassette Library, 1989.
8. Archbishop Rembert G. Weakland OSB, "From Dream to Reality to Vision", *Origins* 20 (11 October, 1990), 293.
9. *Human Sexuality*, p. 27.

Kevin G. Culligan

John of the Cross and modern psychology: A brief journey into the unconscious

The writer was asked to show how John's writings did not contradict psychology but rather prepared the way for it. Not many spiritual writers take the findings of modern psychology seriously enough; many are still suspicious of psychology, it is all too new.

In Book 1 of *The Dark Night*, John of the Cross describes beginners in the spiritual life who are motivated by 'spiritual gluttony'. He writes:

> Some [beginners], attracted by the delight they feel in their spiritual exercises, will kill themselves with penances, and others will weaken themselves by fasts and, without the counsel or command of another, overtax their weakness; indeed they try to hide these penances from the one to whom they owe obedience in such matters. Some will even dare perform these penances contrary to obedience.
>
> Such individuals are unreasonable and most imperfect. They subordinate submissiveness and obedience (which is a penance of reason and discretion, and consequently a sacrifice more pleasing and acceptable to God) to corporal penance. But corporal penance without obedience is no more than a penance of beasts. And like beasts, they are motivated in these penances by an appetite for the pleasure they find in [them] (N 1,6,1-2).

Sigmund Freud could very well have written this description of beginners. What John of the Cross calls a 'penance of beasts', Freud identifies as masochism – inflicting pain on one's body for the sensory pleasure it brings. Freud calls it 'the lust of pain'.[1]

St John also indicates that beginners in the spiritual

life are unaware of the real reason they punish their bodies. Consciously, they think they do this for the honour and glory of God; in reality, "they are motivated in these penances by an appetite for the pleasure they find in them" (N 1,6,2). Freud would say they are unconsciously motivated by the 'pleasure principle'.

For John, this is the major problem for beginners – they are unaware of their real motivation in performing their spiritual exercises. Reading Book 1 of *The Dark Night* where John analyses the behaviour of beginners according to the seven capital sins, one might easily, although wrongly, conclude that beginners are nearly degenerates – proud, avaricious, lustful, angry, gluttonous, envious and slothful. In reality, they have undergone a true conversion, made a firm commitment to serving God, and are very serious about their religious exercises. Their main problem, as John sees it, is their motivation. They think they are serving God by all their prayers, penances and religious practices; in reality, they are seeking the sensory pleasure these religious activities bring them.

In Chapters 2-7 of Book 1 of *The Dark Night* John maintains that the underlying motivation of beginners is the unconscious desire for sensory pleasure. He acknowledges, in fact, that this pleasure is necessary for beginners, "for it is through the delight and satisfaction they experience in prayer and (other religious practices) that they... become detached from worldly things and... (gain) some spiritual strength in God". Nonetheless, John reminds us, "the conduct of these beginners in the way of God is lowly and not too distant from love of pleasure and of self" (N 1,8,3). For this reason, God purifies them of their attachments to self and pleasure so that they might mature religiously and spiritually and seek God in themselves rather than seek themselves in God (A 2,7,5).

This divine purification is the work of contemplation, of both the dark night of sense and the dark night of spirit. Contemplative purification involves, furthermore, an enlightenment by which one becomes increasingly conscious or aware of the true motives for one's behaviour. By the light of contemplation we gradually see God more as God truly is; and we also come to see ourselves more as we truly are. And seeing ourselves as we truly are means having a deep awareness of the true motives for our behaviour. As Freud might put it, our unconscious becomes conscious.

Thus, for the remainder of this talk, I would like to: (i) describe briefly the unconscious from a psychological point of view; (ii) describe St John's understanding of the unconscious; (iii) describe how contemplation heals the unconscious; and (iv) suggest some implications for the relationship between spirituality and psychology.

The unconscious in contemporary psychology

First of all, the unconscious is not a 'thing in itself', but rather a word or a mental construct we use to signify various human phenomena and processes. Open up a person in exploratory surgery and you can locate the heart, the liver, the intestines and most of the internal organs; but you will not find the unconscious, nor the id, nor the ego, nor the superego. These are primarily concepts Freud coined to signify complex human processes. They are valuable only in the degree to which they help us understand and explain these processes.

American psychologists like Carl Rogers and B.F. Skinner did not find Freud's theory of the unconscious particularly helpful for understanding and explaining human behaviour. They discarded it in favour of other mental constructs which they developed – such as operant conditioning and congruence between self and experiencing – which they maintained, on the basis of some disciplined observation and research, better account for human behaviour. Rogers, for example, a direct descendant intellectually of Edmund Husserl's phenomenology, attempted to explain behaviour only from phenomena he could observe in the consulting room or in controlled research, rather than posit entities like the 'unconscious' which could not be observed directly in human phenomena.

For myself, I have had too many lapses of the tongue, too many 'Freudian slips', too many fascinating, and sometimes frightening, dreams to dismiss Freud's theory of the unconscious and its many derivatives which today constitute the field of depth psychology. In fact, I believe Freud's theory of the unconscious is extremely useful in understanding the spiritual life in general and the writings of St John of the Cross in particular.

As a concept, then, the unconscious refers to the human reality that our mental life – our psyche – is far more extensive than that which we are presently aware of, or are aware of at any given moment in our life; moreover, those areas in our mental life of which we are unaware have a dynamic influence on our present behaviour, even though we may not recognise this influence.[2]

Imagine an iceberg, Freud suggested, and you will understand the psyche better. Consciousness is like the tip of the iceberg which we can see above the water; the unconscious, however, is like the rest of the iceberg – and, by far, its greater portion – which is under the water where we cannot see it. Moreover, the unconscious is dynamically connected to the conscious even though we are not aware of it, just as the tip of the iceberg is joined to the rest of the iceberg we cannot see under water.

Another image for the unconscious is an underground storehouse. In it are kept all the experiences one has had since conception. Obviously, all these life experiences cannot be maintained in our conscious mind as we go about our daily activities; were that the case, our minds would simply be overwhelmed with data and we would be unable to function mentally. But these experiences are preserved in the unconscious, where they are potentially available to conscious awareness. Ideally, experiences preserved in the unconscious flow into consciousness at times when they best serve a person's conscious activities. Thus, in a moment of inspiration, the experiences in a poet's unconscious may flow into her consciousness during composition as she strives to find images to express a human experience that has deeply moved her. Problems arise when there have been experiences of conflict and trauma in a person's early life. These conflicts, too, are preserved in the unconscious and can, and often do, influence conscious behaviour.

For example: a young boy is raised by a moralistic and overprotective mother. As he grows older, he becomes increasingly resentful toward her because she so unreasonably restricts his freedom, yet he is unable to express this resentment directly to her for fear of losing her love or being punished by his father. In adulthood, however, this unexpressed or unresolved resentment toward his mother influences his adult life in his passive-aggressive behaviour toward women, although he is now unaware of the direct connection between his feelings toward his mother in childhood and his overt behaviour toward the adult women in his life.

For such cases, Dr Freud prescribed psychoanalysis as the treatment of choice. And following him, depth psychology generally sees the resolution of such problems in psychotherapy or (if you can afford it!) psychoanalysis. By exploring or analysing the man's early life experiences, particularly his relationship with his parents, all of which are 'stored' in his unconscious, the man

89

we are imagining gradually becomes *aware* of the disturbed relationship with his mother and *sees* its connection to his behaviour with the women in his life. As this awareness grows, as the unconscious becomes conscious and the repressed feelings associated with this awareness are 'worked through' in the transference/countertransference process with the therapist, the psychic problem becomes resolved or healed. And the healing consists in this: all the psychic energy that was fixated on the negative interjected image of the mother is released and available for more creative psychic functioning; and, better still, he can now relate to the women in his life as they are in themselves, not as objects for the projection of his unresolved resentment toward his mother.

The implications of Freud's theory of the unconscious for life generally, and for religion in particular, are, of course unlimited. For this reason, William James, writing in *The Varieties of Religious Experience*, considered "the discovery of unconscious states (as) the most important step forward in psychology".[3] Popularly, this discovery is attributed to Sigmund Freud; but, as Lancelot White demonstrates in his book, *The Unconscious Before Freud*,[4] people long before Freud recognised that human beings are motivated in their behaviour by factors they are often totally unaware of. In Christian tradition, St Paul describes a law in his personality which caused him to do what he would prefer not to do (Rom 7:22-23), the Desert Fathers struggled with interior devils, the mediaeval Scholastics knew unconscious motivation, and so on through the history of Christian spirituality, including the writings of St John of the Cross.

John of the Cross and the unconscious

You can discover John's theory of the unconscious if you look closely at those passages where he treats of the

90

memory and of the 'deeply-rooted' disorders in the human soul which are healed by contemplation. For John, memory is a spiritual faculty which, together with intellect and will, enables a person to transcend the boundaries and limitations of the sensory universe and to achieve loving union with the incomprehensible and transcendent God. John pictures the memory as an interior archive or repository. It preserves all the images, fantasies, forms and figures which arise within a person from the impression which the outside world makes upon the five exterior senses (or which God gives to a person supernaturally), together with all the thoughts and ideas produced by the intellect. He describes memory and sensory fantasy with which it is closely associated in this way:

> This interior sense, the fantasy, coupled with the memory, is for the intellect the archives or receptacle (*un archivo y receptaculo del entendimiento*) in which all the intelligible forms and images are received. Like a mirror, this faculty contains them within itself, whether they come to it from the five bodily senses or supernaturally. Not only is the fantasy capable of this, but it can even compose and imagine other objects resembling those known (A 2,16,2).

As this quote indicates, memory is closely associated with the interior sense faculties of imagination and fantasy. These provide the memory with discursive powers, so that it not only preserves images and ideas but also reflects upon them. The memory thus has the power to change or to distort the images and ideas present within it. In addition, emotional attachment to images and ideas carried in the memory, whether accurate or distorted, can give rise to "misgivings, suspicions, disturbances and darknesses" (A 3,3,6) whereas non-attachment to these images and ideas not only bestows interior peace but frees the person to receive the loving knowledge which God communicates in contemplation. For, in addition to receiving the images and ideas of the sense and spirit, the memory, together with the intellect and will, possesses an infinite capacity to receive God's self-communication in contemplation and to have the serenity of God's image impressed upon it (A 1,8,2; F 3,18-22).

Accordingly, John makes this observation regarding the harm the devil can cause through the memory:

> I should like spiritual persons to have full realisation of how many evils the devil causes in souls that make use of their memories; of how much sadness, affliction, vain and evil joy from both spiritual and worldly thoughts these devils occasion; and of the number of impurities they leave *rooted in the spirit*. They also seriously distract these souls from the highest recollection, a recollection which consists of the concentration of all the faculties on the incomprehensible good and the withdrawal of them from all apprehensible things, for these apprehensible things are not a good that is beyond comprehension.
>
> Although the good derived from this void is not as excellent as that arising from the application of the soul to God, by the mere fact it liberates us from a lot of sorrow, affliction and sadness – over and above imperfections and sins – it is an exceptional blessing (A 3,4,2).

The healing of the unconscious

In the foregoing quote, John speaks of "impurities deeply rooted in the spirit". We can gain a deeper understanding of the dynamic but hidden influence which images and ideas preserved over one's entire lifetime in the memory can have upon overt human behaviour by examining more closely the nature of these 'deeply-rooted' disorders in the human soul which need to be healed by contemplation.

In speaking of proficients – those whose prayer is contemplative but who still need to be purified to reach union with God – John writes in Chapter 2 of Book 2 of *The Dark Night*:

> The imperfections in these proficients are of two kinds: habitual and actual.
>
> The habitual are the imperfect affections and habits still remaining like *roots* in the spirit. The difference between the two purgations (– the dark night of sense and the dark night of spirit –) is like the difference between pulling up roots and cutting off a branch... The purgation of the senses is only the gate to and beginning of the contemplation which leads to the purgation of spirit. This sensitive purgation... serves more for the accommodation of the senses to the spirit than for the union of the spirit with God. The stains of the old man still linger in the spirit, *although this may not be apparent or perceptible*. If these are not wiped away by the use of the soap and strong lye of this purgative night, the spirit will be unable to reach the purity of divine union (N 2,2,1).

John notes here that even in contemplatives who have been purified of their pleasure seeking in the dryness of the dark night of sense, there still remain disorders deeply rooted in their spirit of which they are unaware that cause proud, vain, arrogant and self-serving behaviour. He regards this condition as, ultimately, the effect of inherited sin in our lives. Nevertheless, he believes that contemplation heals these disorders deep within the soul.

In *The Dark Night*, Book 2, Chapter 6, John writes:

This contemplation annihilates, empties and consumes all the affections and imperfect habits the person contracted *throughout its life*. Since these imperfections are *deeply rooted* in the substance of the soul, it usually suffers, besides this poverty and this natural and spiritual emptiness, an oppressive undoing and an inner torment (N 2,6,5).

In more graphic language, John describes contemplation as a "divine purge (that) stirs up all the foul and vicious humours of which the person was *never before aware*; never did it realise there was so much evil in itself, since these humours were *so deeply rooted*" (N 2,10,2).

Contemplation heals those deeply-rooted disorders primarily through divine enlightenment. As healing in psychotherapy comes through making the unconscious conscious, so contemplation brings to light the disorders of the soul so that they may be clearly seen, expelled and annihilated. In a passage that sounds descriptive of contemporary psychotherapy, John explains the healing of deep-rooted disorders through the illumination of contemplation. He writes:

At this stage (of contemplative purification) persons suffer from sharp trials in their intellect, severe dryness and distress in their will, and from the burdensome knowledge of their own miseries in their memory, for their spiritual eye gives them a very clear picture of self...
A person's suffering at this time cannot be exaggerated; they are but little less than the sufferings of purgatory... All the person's infirmities are brought to light; they are set before its eyes to be felt and healed (F 1,21).

We note in this passage that through contemplation persons *see* their infirmities, *feel* them and they are healed. As in psychotherapy, the healing of our inner conflicts takes place as we both see them (or they become conscious to us) and feel them. A simple example may help to illustrate this healing process.

There was once a great and holy preacher who was deeply committed to proclaiming God's word 'in season and out'. Although widely recognised for his homiletic achievements, he often felt depressed when other preachers were praised for their sermons. From time to time he would even hear himself damn these preachers with faint praise, much to his own surprise.

One day, while doing his laundry, he asked himself: "Why, if I am so convinced that God's word must be proclaimed, do I become discouraged and jealous when other preachers are praised for doing just that?" Suddenly, it dawned on him. The real motivation for his preaching was to gain recognition for himself, and only secondarily was he concerned with the fate of the Gospel.

As he *saw* his true motivation, he began to *feel* shame and embarrassment for the years he had used the preaching of God's word to promote himself more than God. And yet, when he saw and felt his real motivation, he was able to recommit himself to preaching, now primarily for the sake of the word itself. Subsequently, he also discovered that the success of other preachers no longer depressed him or made him feel jealous; rather, he was able to rejoice that God's word was served through their efforts because their reputation no longer threatened his own self-esteem.

Notice that the preacher's enlightenment came while he was doing his laundry, not when he was in church praying. John understood contemplation to be more a life process that purifies and unites us with God than an extraordinary religious experience that occurs during a special time set aside for prayer. Furthermore, he considered contemplation to be, as Abbot Thomas Keating rightly calls it, 'divine psychotherapy'.[5] This does not mean that contemplation is an inexpensive substitute for psychotherapy: that would misconceive contemplation and devalue psychotherapy. However, it does mean that contemplation, as John of the Cross understood it, is by nature psychotherapeutic – a healing of the psyche – because it enables us to see and feel the effects of sin and the deeply-rooted, unconscious disorders present in our soul.

Purifying the memory

Contemplation, of course, is fundamentally God's work – "a secret and peaceful and loving inflow of God", as John describes it, "which if not hampered, fires the soul in the spirit of love" (N 1,10,6). Nevertheless, there are some things we can do to dispose ourselves for this divine inflow and to avoid hampering its transforming effects in our lives.

In *The Ascent of Mount Carmel*, John teaches that we must learn to free our desires, thoughts, memories and emotions from disordered attachment to created things, and to centre them on God alone if we are to be properly disposed to receive God's healing self-communication in contemplation.

Applying this teaching specifically to the purification of the memory, John gives this advice to spiritual persons in Book 3 of the *Ascent*:

As often as distinct ideas, forms and images occur to persons, they should immediately, without resting in them, turn to God with loving affection, in emptiness of everything that can be remembered. They should not think or look upon these things for a longer time

than is sufficient for the understanding and fulfilment of their obligations, if they refer to this. And
then they should consider these ideas without becoming attached to or seeking gratification in them,
lest they leave their effects in the soul. Thus persons
are not required to cease recalling and thinking about
what they must do and know, for, since they are not
attached to the possession of these thoughts, they
will not be harmed (A 3,15,1).

John's counsel to purify the memory for God amounts
to a simple and gentle 'letting go' of both troubling and
pleasant memories as they come into consciousness.
Letting go of attachments to these specific memories
permits other memories to move freely in and out of our
consciousness and serve our creative activity.

Often, however, it is not easy to let go of troubling
memories or the fear or guilt that may be associated
with earlier life experiences. In such cases, normal daily
functioning may be disturbed and creativity blocked.
Psychotherapeutic intervention is sometimes necessary
to resolve the unconscious conflict which is the source
of the disturbing memories and feelings. Here effective
psychotherapy serves as a helpful, sometimes necessary, adjunct to the contemplative process. Ordinarily,
though, John believed the soul's healing comes principally through the person's continual effort to live in
faith, hope and love and God's gift of contemplation.

This conscious working with our mental activity –
centring our desires, thoughts and emotions in God and
letting go of specific memories – is, you may easily
recognise, the main work of prayer and interior recol-
lection. Our periods of prayer and our continual
mindfulness throughout the day enable us to live in the
present moment and to be continually in touch with the
'first movements' of our desires, thoughts, memories
and emotions and quite gently to bring this mental ac-

tivity into harmony with our abiding effort to be open to God's transforming love.

Often we appear, even to ourselves, to be doing nothing, to be empty, mentally, emotionally and spiritually; yet, this non-attachment to desires, ideas, memories and emotions is an effective way of 'not hindering' God's healing work in our lives. John of the Cross provides a most compelling image, taken from the Gospel, which helps us to persevere in this practice. Discussing the purification of the memory through hope in *The Ascent of Mount Carmel*, Book 3, John writes:

> The person should remain closed (to all attachments to thoughts, memories and feelings), then, without care or afflictions, for he who entered the room of his disciples bodily, while the doors were closed (without their knowing how this was possible), and gave them peace, will enter the soul spiritually (without its knowing how or using any effort of its own), once it has closed the doors of its intellect, memory and will to all apprehensions. And he will fill them with peace, descending upon them, as the prophet says, like a river of peace (Is,66:12). In this peace he will remove all the misgivings, suspicions, disturbances and darknesses that made the soul fear it had gone astray. The (person) should persevere in prayer and hope in the midst of nakedness and emptiness, for its blessing will not be long in coming (A 3,3,6).

In addition to being the source of interior peace, this way of being present to God also appears to best dispose us to receive the creative inflowing from our unconscious – the underground storehouse of all our personal experiences and even, as Jung believed, the experience of the entire human family – into our conscious mental life. John of the Cross suggests this when he describes persons who have been transformed in God. He writes:

These persons... perform only fitting and reasonable works, and none that are not so. For God's spirit makes them know what must be known and ignore what must be ignored, remember what ought to be remembered – with or without forms – and forget what ought to be forgotten, and makes them love what they ought to love, and keeps them from loving what is not in God. Accordingly, all the first movements of these faculties (of intellect, memory and will) are divine. And it is no wonder that the movements and operations of these faculties are divine, for they are transformed in divine being (A 3,2,9).

John calls contemplation the 'inflow of God' into human life, a life-long process by which God enlightens us to see more clearly not only who God is but also who we are. God, then, even more than a 'transformed consciousness', is the goal or end of this contemplative process. For John assures us that, after God's light has revealed to us and healed the deep-rooted disorders that sin and life experience have left in our unconscious, God awakens in the depths of our being to welcome us in an embrace of transforming love. Commenting on the last stanza of his poem, *The Living Flame of Love*, John describes this awakening in the depths of our soul.

How gentle and loving (that is, extremely loving and gentle) is your awakening, O Word, Spouse, in the centre and depth of my soul, which is its pure and intimate substance, in which secretly and silently, as its only lord, you dwell alone, not only as in your house, nor only as in your bed, but also as in my own heart, intimately and closely united to it. And how delicately you captivate me and arouse my affections towards you in the sweet breathing you produce in this awakening, a breathing delightful to me and full of good and glory (F 4,3).

Thus, for John, the purification of the memory and the healing of the unconscious through contemplation are not merely for the sake of a relatively conflict-free and creative human consciousness (which was Freud's goal in psychoanalysis) but ultimately for the union of the whole person with God present in its 'deepest centre' in lively faith, hope and love.

Conclusions and implications

In the preceding pages, I have compared Sigmund Freud and John of the Cross on the subject of the unconscious. I have attempted to show that what Freud accounted for in his theory of the unconscious, namely, the preservation of life experiences and the hidden, but dynamic, psychic processes which affect overt human behaviour, John covers in his treatment of memory and the deep-rooted disorders of the human soul. I have also tried to show that both writers see the healing of the unconscious as coming through enlightenment, in making the unconscious conscious. For Freud, this healing by enlightenment is a result of psychoanalysis; in John, it comes through contemplation. Although John's view of the human person as a harmonious composite of sense and spirit (N 2,11,4; C 16,5 and 10) is wider and deeper than Freud's biologically determined understanding of the human, both nonetheless attempt to explain unconscious motivation and the healing of the soul, two of our most important, and puzzling, human questions.

This interest of Freud and John of the Cross in the same critical areas of human life suggests that the disciplines of Carmelite spirituality and contemporary psychology ought to remain in close dialogue. Those especially who practise the fine arts of spiritual direction and psychotherapy have much to learn from one another. Contemporary psychology, for example, has continued Freud's interest in the unconscious and pursued extensively its bio-physical, psycho-personal, sociocultural and transpersonal-spiritual implications. As "the various fields of psychology continue to study that which influences our behaviour, but of which we are not aware,[6] their findings most certainly will be enormously valuable to spiritual directors whose work, as John of the Cross points out in the first book of *The Dark Night*, often focuses upon helping persons understand the true motives for their religious behaviour. In particular, psychological research into the unconscious can help us fully appreciate John of the Cross's remarkable insight that memory includes not simply what can be easily called forth into consciousness (what Freud would call the preconscious) but all life experiences which are somewhere retained in the human organism and which subtly influence our behaviour. Finally, the ongoing psychological research into determining precisely the healing factors in psychotherapy has direct implications for spiritual directors as they assist people to grow into wholeness through prayer and Christian living.

On the other hand, Carmelite spirituality can assist contemporary psychology continually to expand its vision of the human beyond its current models of personality to include the human person's infinite capacity for transcendent truth, goodness and beauty – ultimately for God. From their own experience in working with persons, spiritual directors can point to the healing effects of prayer and meditation, of faith and hope particularly for the healing of the unconscious, and the mysterious healing power of the cross when freely accepted. Because of the person's infinite capacity for God, yet the continuous effects of sin upon human choice, Christian spirituality can help psychotherapists appreciate that a human person is not fully healed when emotional fixations on certain introjected objects have been released. Much more still remains to restore a person to wholeness which is ultimately achieved when the human person is transformed in God.

For these reasons, it greatly benefits human persons when their psychotherapists and spiritual directors collaborate directly with one another. Through their regular consultation, referral of a person to one another or working conjointly with the same person as need may dictate, psychotherapists and spiritual directors together can provide invaluable assistance in helping persons to recover the wholeness God intends for his people which was lost through sin.

My own experience firmly convinces me that such dialogue and mutual collaboration as I have suggested here between Carmelite spirituality and contemporary psychology, between spiritual directors and psychotherapists, will assist both disciplines to pursue more effectively their common goal, which Jesus Christ articulated as 'the fullness of life'.

NOTES

1. Nandor Fodor and Frank Gaynor (eds) *Freud: Dictionary of Psychoanalysis*, Greenwich, Connecticut: Fawcett Publications, Inc., 1958, pp. 93-4.
2. Horace B. English and Ava C. English, *A Comprehensive Dictionary of Psychological and Psychoanalytical Terms*, New York: David MacKay Co., Inc., 1958, pp. 569-70.
3. Quoted in Natalino Caputi, *Guide to the Unconscious*, Birmingham, Alabama: Religious Education Press, 1984, p. 1.
4. Lancelot L. Whyte, *The Unconscious Before Freud*, New York: Basic Books, 1960.
5. Thomas Keating ocso, "Contemplation, the Divine Therapy", Part IV (six one-hour tapes) of *The Spiritual Journey: A Contemporary Presentation of Christian Growth and Transformation*, 3rd revised and enlarged edition, Colorado Springs, Colorado: Contemporary Communications, 1989.
6. Caputi, *Guide*, p. 155.

Richard Copsey

John
and spiritual discernment

There is such a need for discernment today, perhaps more than at any other stage in the history of the Church. There is so much that is good in the Church today but there is also much confusion and error.

This lecture comes after twenty years of studying St John of the Cross, trying to understand his writings, and attempting to live religious life in his shadow – and I still feel that I have not even come close to him.

To start with I want to look at three significant episodes in the life of John in order to get the framework right. I am totally at one with what Ron Rolheiser said earlier in this congress about John being from earliest years a man of prayer. However, I hesitate to use the word 'mystic' to describe him when a child. I will come back to that because it is a word that has so many connotations. My tendency is to reserve it for certain specific experiences. Clearly, for his earliest years, both as a young boy and then as a student, John had a very intense personal prayer life. But we would misunderstand him if we thought that, as a youth, he had in mind that he was going to write *The Ascent of Mount Carmel* and *The Dark Nigh tof the Soul* or that he would spend a large part of his life talking to nuns and lay people about prayer. I think that any such idea was very far from his thoughts. In reality, John was somewhat of a recluse in his early years. He was always going off on his own to find a secluded corner in which to pray quietly by himself. Somebody asked about whether John of the Cross would have had any girl friends. I have to say that, from all I have read, it is very unlikely. John was too much of a 'loner'.

By the time he joined the Carmelites in 1563, John was clearly seeking a secluded life of prayer and contemplation; he saw the Carmelites as a religious order which could provide that. His novitiate was spent in the Carmelite house in Medina del Campo which had been founded not long before, so the community there was probably still enthusiastic and faithful to their Rule. I think the sad thing is that when he went to Salamanca, he began to despair of finding a contemplative life with Carmelites of the Ancient Observance. On the other hand, it has to be admitted that as a young man, John was not always the easiest person to live with. In Salamanca, when he was appointed prefect of studies, his fellow students were heard to say as he came down the corridor, "Look, here comes that devil! Let's be off." John was evidently very strict and single-minded in his commitment to his religious vocation.

The first of the three seminal episodes which changed the life of John occurred in 1567. After John had been ordained in Salamanca, he returned to Medina del Campo to celebrate his first Mass before his mother and family. During this visit, he met Teresa of Avila and this chance meeting led to a major change in his whole life. At this time, John was thinking of becoming a Carthusian and burying himself in a monastic cell, quietly concentrating on coming closer to God. It was through the encounter with Teresa that God was able to reach out to John and, as it were, pluck him by the hair of his head and propel him in a different direction. It is Teresa who tells him: "No, the Carthusian life is not for you. A reform movement has started within the Carmelite order and we are going to establish houses which will provide the opportunities for prayer and the contemplative life which you are seeking. That is where you are needed." Here is an example of a prophet being told what to do by a woman. It reminds me of the wedding feast at Cana when the hosts ran out of wine and Jesus asked: "What has this got to do with me?" And his mother told him! For John, this meeting with Teresa was one of the pivotal points in his life.

The second significant experience for John was his imprisonment in Toledo. It is a sorry episode and reflects badly on the religious politics of the day. But, in a sense, we have got to read God's purpose in it the same way that we read the crucifixion. You see, if it had not been for Christ's crucifixion, we would never have had the redemption and, similarly, the imprisonment in Toledo was for John a sort of crucifixion. It was an experience which created the setting in which he could attain a height in prayer which otherwise he might never have reached. I know there were all sorts of political and malicious reasons why John was imprisoned although please do not believe all the horror stories that you read about how he was treated during his imprisonment. There is little contemporary description of his period in prison; most written accounts actually describe what might have happened or, more specifically, what was permitted by the Constitutions. There is no doubt that John was very much isolated, under persuasion from an aggressive and antagonistic Carmelite community who tried to get him to give up the reform. Being locked up in a small cell with very little light – he could only read his breviary by holding it high up – created an environment which almost threw John into mystical prayer. The sheer despair – and I think there were periods of near despair in Toledo or moments when he came very close to it – created the opening through which God could reach John at a level that he had never spoken to him before. It is while he is in prison in Toledo that John felt the need to express his experience of prayer in some way. There are obvious practical reasons why John could not write a book at the time but, more importantly, the experience he had was beyond any simple description. So the compulsion to describe his experiences begins to draw out of John a new way of expressing himself through his poetry. If you can describe an experience in words, then, in some fashion, even if it is somewhat symbolic or vague, you can hold on to it and begin to make sense of it. For John, as he begins quietly in the dark in his prison in Toledo, composing his poetry is a way of holding on to the experience of God. His poetry contains some strong, sexual imagery and this is largely derived from his knowledge of the Song of Songs, a classic text at the time for anybody involved in talking about prayer. I have recently been counting up the number of English Carmelites who wrote commentaries on the Bible before the Reformation and the Song of Songs was clearly the most popular book in the Old Testament for them.

There is a third experience, not so much as episode but a climate which significantly changed John. It happened after his escape from Toledo. To prevent recapture, John travelled south and, for the first few months, he stayed in El Calvario – a small, isolated Carmelite community. Every weekend, he would go across to the nuns in Beas to hear confessions and give them spiritual talks. Now, it is my opinion that the nuns in Beas deserve a special medal for the way in which they encouraged John to reveal himself. Initially, they probably asked: "What was it like in Toledo?" However, John was not the sort of person to spend time describing his personal sufferings nor how he was punished. Yet the nuns caught a glimpse of the fact that he had written some poetry. So, being typical nuns, they said, "Please read your poetry to us." And John began to recite his poetry. Then, like many a present-day Carmelite community, the nuns demanded, "May we have some more. Please, can you explain what it means." And John would have realised that he needed to explain his poetry. There are nuns sitting there, waiting for him, eager to learn more about prayer. And it is from this point that John starts first to talk about the higher levels of prayer and then to write his books. From then onwards, in El Calvario, Baeza and especially Granada, there will be communities of reformed Carmelite nuns demanding: "Tell us about prayer. Read us some of your poetry. Can you explain what it means?"

I am reminded here of a retreat I gave to a community of Carmelite sisters. During it, I gave them three talks of St John of the Cross which exhausted my prepared material. They asked me for more! So, I had to sit down and think of something further to say. Somehow I managed it, but afterwards I uttered a sincere thank you to the sisters because their request had drawn out of me ideas about John and prayer which I had never expressed before, concepts which until then I did not know that I knew. I think this is similar to the way that the nuns drew out of John teachings about prayer which probably he did not realise that he knew. I am tempted to think that when John got to the end of writing *The Ascent of Mount Carmel* and *The Dark Night of Spirit*, he said; "Good heavens, did I actually write that?" The nuns created a climate, a stimulating audience. They were eager to know, keen to learn, hanging on every word that John uttered, appreciating what he had to offer. And this effect needs to be taken into account because, had John been allowed to go his own way, he would probably have ended up as a Carthusian passing his life quietly in a cell and we would have heard no more of him. The *digitus Dei*, the finger of God, was at work in these circumstances, prodding, pushing and stimulating him.

Now, what about these nuns to whom John was talking in Beas while he was recovering after Toledo? They were obviously enthusiastic, a new community dedicated to the Carmelite reform and wishing to learn about prayer. They had probably learnt about formal meditation during their novitiate but the experience that comes in prayer is that meditation takes us only so far. After a while, we need to put the Bible or meditation book on one side and simply share with God. Prayer becomes a talking to God, a discourse. This opening of ourselves to God is sustained by a real feeling of his presence, a sense of his closeness. And then this desire to share, to talk, diminishes. We end up, as it were, balanced in front of God, tongue-tied, not wanting to say anything. If you read the *Spiritual Letters*[1] of Dom Chapman – he was the Benedictine Abbot of Downside in 1920's – he calls this experience, the 'ligature'. It is as if God holds on to us, stops us uttering anything. We find ourselves suspended in front of God, not wanting to say anything and, if you do try to force words, it all seems a waste of time and distraction of attention. All we want is to focus ourselves on God and remain there with him. This is probably the experience that many of the nuns were encountering in Beas. Dom Chapman reckoned that any religious should reach this point within six months. Please do not think that I want to limit this description to religious nuns but they were the people for whom John was writing initially. The experience of prayer is no different for any one else although religious are rather lucky in that, frequently, they have more time for prayer. The experience is common to anyone who tries to live a life of prayer; John wrote in a similar fashion to the lay people who sought his advice.

It is important to note that the demands on John for spiritual direction after Toledo were different to the demands that he had in Avila. In 1572, he had been invited by Teresa to go to Avila to help reform the convent there. This community had almost been the despair of the Prior General, Rossi, during his visitation of Spain in 1567. There were about 130 nuns in the convent and not enough food to go round. In fact, Teresa, after becoming prioress, boasted that she never ate at the common table. The reason was that she did not want to be a burden on the community; depriving them of a portion of food. Teresa had her food sent in by her friends. At the time of the visitation, the Prior General forbade the community to accept any more novices because they were unable to feed the existing community. When Teresa herself became prioress in 1571 with the task of reforming the community, her entry was strongly resisted. The Carmelite Provincial and the Mayor of Avila found all the doors locked when they accompanied Teresa to the convent. Teresa only managed to make her entry by squeezing through a side door. Once inside, she was faced with a large number of nuns who resented her appointment. So, as part of her strategy to win them over and improve the quality of religious life, she asked for John of the Cross to be one of the chaplains for the convent. John found that many of the nuns had drifted away from religious life, often it was simply the sheer poverty of the house that forced them to fend for themselves. So his main effort was to encourage the community to return to the full observance of contemplative life. His efforts were remarkably successful. Within a few years, he had acquired a tremendous reputation for holiness and skill in spiritual direction.

However, after his imprisonment in Toledo and the developing success of the reform movement, John was meeting nuns at Beas, Baeza and Granada, who had already accepted the reform and who were dedicated and eager to develop their personal prayer life. So he was not so much worried about them following the religious life as describing to them how the life of prayer develops.

The fundamental principle of John's teaching is that we have to learn how to give ourselves totally, utterly and completely to God. We have to learn how to direct ourselves towards God. This desire involves a single-mindedness and a dedication. We have to set up a lifestyle, a framework within which we live, which facilitates a real prayer life with God. Prayer is not something that we can turn to and forget everything else. Prayer is our love of God, the top of the pyramid, built on all the actions that we did during the rest of the day. John talks about training ourselves in all spheres. We have, of course, read those stern commands which John writes in Book 1 Chapter 13 of *The Ascent of Mount Carmel*:

> Endeavour to be inclined always:
> not to the easiest, but the most difficult;
> not to the most delightful, but to the harshest...[2]

However, I do not think John meant this quite as strongly as we tend to read it today. He really is not a stern forbidding character. If we want to know about John and his teaching, then we should start with the biographies of him – these give us a flavour of his personality – and then read his letters. John is quite different in the letters – he is really warm, loving and gentle. And this was the experience of the nuns in Avila – they found him so kind and encouraging. Yet his books almost put us off. We need to realise, as well, that John was writing textbooks for learning about prayer. It was Teresa who was writing the novels. There is a historical reason for the difference. John came from a very poor background and when he was growing up there were probably no books at all in his home. Although he was well educated by the Jesuits, it is unlikely that he had any opportunity of reading fiction or romances. I get the feeling that John read most books simply in order to get from A to B; they were like textbooks to pass exams with, to be read before examinations. His great love was the Bible and here he was unrivalled in his knowledge. He read other spiritual works, such as *The Golden Epistle*[3] by William of St Thiery but any work which was not religious was for John simply a distraction, an irrelevance. Now Teresa was exactly the opposite. As a child, she enjoyed reading novels and was fascinated by stories of the Moors and acts of heroism, etc. So, when Teresa writes, she has the image of a romantic novel and her works tell an exciting story. With John, it is different. He puts down the facts, explains points and concentrates on getting ideas across. In essence, it is a textbook. So, we need to take this into account.

When John writes: "... be inclined always, not to the easiest, but to the most difficult...", he is teaching us that we must follow God without being distracted by whether our tasks are pleasurable or not. The simplest way to understand his approach is to take the example of how young squires were trained in the mediaeval period. Squires needed to be able to fight in battle and especially how to fight with the sword. So, when they were old enough, they would be given a wooden sword which was about twice the weight of a normal sword. With this wooden sword, they learnt all the cuts, thrusts and parries needed in sword-fighting. After they had developed these basic skills, they were then introduced to a normal, steel sword. You can imagine their response to the lighter weapon. At once, everything appeared so much easier and they acquired real confidence. Another example is the athlete who is preparing for a one-mile race. In his practice sessions, he doesn't just run one mile, he runs three, four or five miles. He knows that when the race occurs, his extra training will pay off and one mile will seem so much easier and simpler. John's teaching is something similar but for the spiritual life. He wants us to choose tasks which we find difficult or unpleasant and do them deliberately. He knows that if we repeat this approach and train ourselves then we will arrive at the stage where it does not matter if a task is easy or not. What will matter is whether God wants it done. Any difficulty is irrelevant. I do not think John is being masochistic; he is saying that when we train ourselves we have to push ourselves harder in order to make sure that we have the strength there when it is needed. Later on when we are being called by God to do things, we won't be dissuaded from doing them because they are unpleasant, we will do them because God is asking us.

Returning to the nuns in Beas, I think they had moved past the stage of formal meditation and were experiencing the desire to stay silent, in front of God. However, the advice that they would probably have received from most traditional confessors was that sitting passively before God was mere idleness. Many priests would have encouraged them to return to meditation or to concentrate on vocal prayers such as the rosary. For the nuns, seeking to develop a real contemplative life, this advice must have been galling. John of the Cross was one of the first people that they had met who understood about prayer. He would have taught them that the prayer of simple adoration is a normal experience in religious life and one step on the road to union with Christ. John encouraged them to persist and, through his knowledge of prayer, helped them to make further progress.

In his day, John had to be especially careful in his teaching on prayer. The prevalent heresy was Quietism – a doctrine which asserted that all you needed to do in prayer was to sit passively, doing nothing and letting God do everything. Now John does not teach this at all but people could listen to him and easily pick phrases out of his writings and accuse him of Quietism. After his death, his writings were suspect and it took time for people to fully appreciate his balanced, orthodox approach.

John's teaching is quite different. He shows us that this darkness, this quietness is part of God's plan for us. We have to wait in the stillness before God. I think in this respect that we may need to change John's terminology. When we pray, we pray with the totality of ourselves. Too often, we think that only our head does the praying or only the heart is praying but we pray with all of ourselves. This morning, perhaps we were in chapel trying to pray but getting distracted, the sun in your eyes, wondering what the talk today was going to be like or what is on the menu for lunch. We might have thought that we were not praying at all and I think that many of the Carmelite nuns in Spain would have posed the same question to John. An essential part of what John is trying to get across is that we pray with the wholeness of ourselves, our whole body speaks for us and the fact that we are in the chapel and we are quiet, then our arms, our hands, our legs and all of us speak to God saying how we want to be close to him. So, even if our mind goes racing around on errands of its own, it is only a part of us. Someone once said that a distraction in prayer is only a bright idea occurring at the wrong time! Remaining in quietness and stillness before God is almost like a balancing act. It is Thomas Merton in his poem *The Quickening of St John the Baptist*[4] who talks about contemplatives as being "planted like sentinels upon the world's frontier", watching out for the coming of God. I think that is an accurate image of prayer. In the darkness and stillness, we watch and wait for the presence of God to bring us to life.

Watching and waiting in the darkness of prayer then we are open to all sorts of problems and this is where John is the supreme master. He has an uncanny knack for explaining the problems and difficulties that we face. It is in the stillness of contemplative prayer that imagination can so easily lead us astray. To show you how easy it is, let me give an illustration. The English Carmelite province owns a mediaeval castle in Kent called Allington Castle complete with moat and battlements. If I were to invite you there tonight, show you to your room up a long, winding staircase at the top of one of the towers, bid you 'Goodnight' and leave you alone there, I bet that many of you would find the experience quite frightening. Can you imagine being left alone in a strange room in an old, unknown building? It would be easy to be startled by the slightest creak, to imagine 'someone' coming along the corridor. On one occasion, we had some voluntary workers there who sat up late telling each other ghost stories until, in the end, they were so frightened that they could not go back to their rooms! Now imagination can play tricks on us in prayer in a not dissimilar way. After all, we are only human. We can easily begin to think that God is revealing himself to us. We can imagine that small sounds in the night are God whispering to us. Some people imagine all sorts of things and this is where John's teaching is so clear and so understanding. He explains that, although we may imagine God talking to us or that there are special revelations happening, special visions or something, in reality, these are simply the effects of our imagination which deflect us away from God. Our purpose in prayer is to hold ourselves there in front of God, opening ourselves to him. We must not be led away. John teaches that the important thing is not to worry about the effects of what is happening nor the experience that we are going through but to keep our concentration fixed on God. Even if an angel appears, John cautions us to ignore him (or her). The angel may be sent by God or he may be sent by the devil but essentially he is only a distraction. We need to concentrate our mind and stay with God himself. That is the important thing.

John also teaches us that we should not let other things distract us either. We may prefer praying in a particular place – a favourite oratory or chapel; John cautions us that that can become a fixation. Possibly, we have a special crucifix or rosary, something of sentimental value, or a statue by which we always pray. John shows us how these can be distractions from God himself, a clinging on to material supports. There comes a moment when we need to push them out of the way.

Our task is to aim ourselves at God alone. At our Carmelite priory at Aylesford, a shrine to Our Lady, we meet many people who are sure that they can feel the presence of God there. They can sense a holiness in the air. Those of us who live in the community at Aylesford know that the reality is not as simple. People get so caught up in places and things. John works steadily on us, paring us away from all these attachments. For him prayer is not about an experience nor the feelings that we have. There is a phrase that I use, not one of John's I'm afraid but I think he would approve of it: "In prayer it is not our experience that matters, it is God's experience; it's not whether we feel happier when we come out of prayer that is important, it is whether God feels happier." Figuratively speaking, we have to ask ourselves whether God has got a smile on his face when we finish our prayer. If he has, then that's real prayer. It is a question of changing the focus of our attention away from what we are experiencing to what God is experiencing. Is our prayer a real act of love and worship?

John is also very perceptive in recognising the secondary processes that take place cloaked by the label 'prayer'. For example, to call oneself a contemplative can be a sort of status symbol. It is not uncommon to have someone coming for spiritual direction who starts off by saying: "I have great graces in prayer, Father." In a sense, it's a way of drawing attention to oneself. John recognises this very clearly and he had a great talent for seeing through our pretences. There are other ways in which the label 'prayer' can serve secondary ends. Seeking spiritual guidance can represent a way of establishing a relationship, a friendship with another person. Or, for example, the discovery of a 'spiritual problem' can provide a way of getting attention. Alternatively, if we want to get attention without having a specific problem, then we can say that we have mystical experiences!

Sadly, some people need these stratagems in order to gain attention and support.

John is fully aware that these activities can take place and his descriptions in his writings are very perceptive. Of course, a claim to contemplative prayer can cloak more seriously disturbed patterns of behaviour. Contemplative prayer provides great opportunities for people who are psychologically disturbed. We have to accept that talk of mystical experiences can act as a magnet to some people, a ready content for people who suffer from mental illness. There are two words which are useful to differentiate here: process and content. The content of what somebody says is not the most important aspect; it is the psychological process that is taking place. A somewhat cynical phrase I employed when training counsellors was, "Don't listen to what the client says; watch what they are up to."

There are times that we will meet people who talk about visions. We have to accept that schizophrenics with hallucinations who believe in God will tend to have visions with a religious content. Atheistic schizophrenics tend to worry more about mysterious rays coming out of the television set or nuclear radiation. Hysterics who believe in God will often have their hysterical symptoms full of religious imagery. They will be 'slain in the spirit' or have a 'conversion experience'. Neurotic people who are centred on religion will possibly have neurotic scruples. What is important here is not the content of what someone is saying but the psychological process which is taking place. John, a man of the sixteenth century, did not use these terms but I think in his writings he was very conscious of the distinction. He was very much aware that you had to read behind what the person was saying to what they were trying to do.

Similarly, if you hear reports of miracles, visions, stigmata, etc., John gives some very reasonable advice on them too. He advises us to leave them alone; as far as he is concerned they represent distractions, they draw us away from giving attention to God himself. He would advise us to put all our effort into living quietly and faithfully in the presence of God.

And that is the simple intention of all of us as we try to come closer to God. As we turn to him, we need to concentrate solely on him and focus all our attention on him. If we are trying to be a person of prayer then we can gain great benefit from what John teaches us. If we hold to him as we walk through the dark night of prayer, then we will have a very sure guide to show us the way. I know his guidance and his intercession for us will help us draw ever closer to God himself.

NOTES

1. *The Spiritual Letters of Dom Chapman* osb, London: Sheed & Ward, 1935, repr. 1969, 61 and other passages.
2. *Collected Works of St John of the Cross*, trans. Kieran Kavanagh ocd and Otilio Rodriguez ocd, Washington: Institute of Carmelite Studies, 1979, 102.
3. William of St Thiery, *The Golden Epistle*, Michigan: Cistercian Publications, 1971. Note: This book was used as a standard text on prayer in Carmelite novitiates of the period.
4. *The Collected Poems of Thomas Merton*, London: Sheldon Press, 1978, 199-202.

Ursula Fleming

John and pain

A very common experience in life today is pain. The essay is an attempt to show how John can help us all at such times when he speaks not of pain as such but the 'Dark Night', which is a symbol.

In common with other people now, I am scared to travel on the London underground. I get claustrophobic and I am assailed by horror at the sheer ugliness of it.

We have accustomed ourselves to thinking that travelling underground is a normal thing to do but the truth is that we go down into the bowels of the earth; darkly, and in vile noise. We are carried, jerking like the peristaltic action of the bowel itself, from one station to the next until spewed out, if we are lucky, at the one we want. If not we could be vomited up anywhere along the line or, alternatively, locked in unmoving, constipated agony for anything up to five hours.

Since the fire at Kings Cross which exploded through the hall of the station eating, killing everything in its path, travelling by tube has become a nightmare. I have actually seen flames coming from under a moving train. Announcements are made over the Tannoy ordering immediate evacuation of trains and stations. It is, to anyone with an imagination, a primitive descent into hell.

But – if you lift your head and raise your eyes to read, from boredom or any other motive, the advertisements, sometimes witty, sometimes gross, near the roof of the train, among them you will see a verse of poetry – unadorned, with no comment, just one verse and the name of the author. It is like a flower growing out of concrete. It is a reminder of heaven while you are in hell. The intensity of the pleasure it gives can lift you into a realm of glory unexperienced in the monochrome, daily life of the city. I rarely feel a similar intensity or spontaneity even in response to the works of art in the museums or art galleries around the place.

They are too safe, too protected, too clinical. I am too safe, too protected, too clinical. My brain takes over and it is an effort to stop myself from analysing, being clever, competing.

Suffering, fear, discomfort, pain can act as a catalyst freeing you from the mediocre mud of humdrum experience into a world of intensity where colours are richer, sounds resound, rhythms explode. Into the life of poetry. And, if you are John, beyond that into the knowledge of God and his presence.

John's poetry flowered from his pain. The intensity of his suffering brought about a density of experience which could only be expressed in the concentrated form of poetry.

In the commentaries, he tried to translate these experiences into a less compacted form extending into hundreds of pages what the poetry said in very few. He says some wonderful things in the commentaries but you have to look for them.

In the first page of the *Ascent* he said, "The darkness and trials, spiritual and temporal, that fortunate souls ordinarily encounter on their way to the high state of perfection are so numerous and profound that human science cannot understand them adequately... He who suffers them will know what it is like but he will find himself unable to describe it."

The poem of *The Dark Night* is not descriptive. You stand outside when you describe something, looking for the right words to use. John was wholly inside the experience when he wrote *The Dark Night*.

He said that "Human science cannot adequately understand the darkness and trials that fortunate souls encounter on their way to the high state of perfection." Human science didn't understand them then. It doesn't understand them now. And now it doesn't even recognise that there is a high state of perfection to reach for.

Leriche says: "Pain is the resultant of the conflict between the stimulus and the individuals." "It is not simply a physical sensation," says Twycross, "it is a dual phenomenon, one being the perception of the sensation and the other the person's emotional reaction to it."

We all know what pain is because in varying degrees we have all suffered it. But it is not an entity in itself. It is indeed 'nothing'. It is a reaction. If you dissect a cadaver you can see and touch the eyeball or the ear and trace the nerves from them leading to the brain but there is no tangible part of the body which can be called pain.

And our reactions to it are all different. It is interesting because if you immerse two peoples' hand in cold water and then add ice until it is freezing both will classify the sensation as painful when the T'o reaches a certain point, but one may be yelling and pulling his hand away where the other is calm and at peace. And if you said to both, "I will fry your child alive in front of your eyes if you move your hand", they will probably feel no pain at all and leave their hands in the water indefinitely. Within limits and with help and very humbly it is possible to control pain as I am sure John himself knew.

The physiological mechanism whereby we can control pain has not been sufficiently researched. It is to do with the secretion of endorphins, a self-anaesthetising hormone produced by the body. By everyone's body. A true gift of God. But if you are self-engrossed and in a state of tension it doesn't work. The prospect of your child tortured in your presence makes you forget your feelings completely so you relegate the sensation of pain into an unimportant category. The pain no longer matters to you. So you don't feel it.

This is the crux of the matter. Literally, if your life, your comfort, your happiness are all important to you then, when any of these are under threat, you become frightened, you will fight, your body will become tense like that of a hedgehog under attack and the pain you suffer will co-relate to the intensity of the fear you undergo. "Love casteth out fear." If your trust in God is sufficient to cast out your fear – of deprivation, of extinction, of whatever – acute pain releases primitive fears you never even knew existed; if your trust is in the true God, you repel the fake god of panic and your pain is eased.

Another example of how this self-anaesthetising process works is sometimes seen after a traumatic accident or in sport. Often a footballer plays on in a match unaware that his leg has been broken until the excitement of the game is over. He has no time to think about himself at all.

John's pain increased the intensity of his trust in God.

> In experiencing the troublesome presence of the enemy, the soul enters more deeply into its inner depths without knowing how and without any efforts of its own, and it is sharply aware of being placed in a certain refuge when it is more hidden and withdrawn from the enemy. There the peace and joy which the devil planned to undo increases. All that fear remains outside, and the soul exults in a very clear consciousness of secure joy in the quiet peace and delight of the hidden spouse which neither the world nor the devil can either give or take away. He is aware of this strength and peace even though he frequently feels that outside his flesh and bones are being tormented (*The Dark Night*, p. 383).

John felt God's mercy as his pain was eased. He realised that by his reaction to pain he either increased

or subdued it. The pain remained but it became toler-
able and harmless:

> Neither the devil nor temporal nor rational things...
> can do harm to the man who walks in faith (*The
> Ascent*, p. 107).

Suffering is not a punishment from God.

John recognised in it a process of learning which has
great value. He described the souls encountering pain
as being 'the fortunates' because they are given the
opportunity to learn.

I work as a practising Catholic in a London teaching
hospital. It is not fashionable to be Catholic and many of
the intelligent surgeons who deride me for my naivety
in believing in God say, in protest, "How can a good
God allow the suffering we see here every day?"

John worked in a hospital too and he affirmed that
God not only allowed suffering but that those who suffered pain were among the fortunates. He said that the
process of reaching union with God is a painful one. It is
a process of discarding selfish things, of changing oneself. And change itself is painful. Like the child emerg-
ing from the womb. Like the butterfly from the chrysalis
or the snake shedding its old skin. Pain, whether it be
physical or mental, brings about a change – if we use
intelligence, if we work at it. We have the choice. Either
we react automatically with fear and tension like a hedgehog and make it worse, or we work at understanding
what it is in us that exacerbates, even sometimes causes
pain – fear, tension, self-absorption all stemming from
over preoccupation with self and lack of trust in the
mercy of God. If you let go into that mercy and truly
trust in God you lose fear, find peace and your pain is
eased.

Spiritual truths can be tested by comparison with
their physical and psychological counterparts. The

fortunates according to John are those who suffer pain; the less fortunate, then, are those whose lifestyle is pain-free; but those who are unfortunate, by everyone's standards, are those who are born unable to feel pain. Their joints become fixed and deformed because the onset of pain does not warn them to move during sleep as we must. They burn themselves without knowing. In childhood they have been known to poke out the eyeballs. They walk on fractured limbs until again deformation sets in. These unfortunates, deprived of pain, live in a half-life and die before their time. The cause of their early death is loss of the ability to feel pain.

Those who can't feel emotional pain, the psychopaths, are equally deprived. They can neither be hurt themselves nor can they understand others' hurt. They are the mass murderers – the criminals who hardly understand the meaning of crime.

Patients who have been prescribed long-term tranquillisers describe the effects as becoming like a zombie – neither happy nor unhappy because they are unable to feel. The effort and the agony they suffer in order to free themselves of tranquilliser addiction testify to how awful it must be. Pain is a teacher. Perhaps *the* teacher. Without it we repeat the same mistakes time after time. If a child doesn't feel the pain of falling, it will take a long time to learn to walk. Those congenitally unable to feel pain don't learn to correct their behaviour or to change and grow as God wants us to. We who feel pain are the fortunate. We should be grateful. In childhood John suffered both physical and mental pain. He suffered all the pain induced by poverty. When he was six, for two years he suffered the pain of watching his father sicken and die and then he suffered bereavement. He had to help his mother to work and support the family. He must have felt hungry and continually tired. The carefree element of childhood can never have been his. He had to learn to survive.

His life in Carmel was comparatively undistinguished until his imprisonment when he was ritualistically beaten each week by his own brethren, when he was left in darkness and alone, starved and filthy. It was then and after that that he wrote his poetry.

It is not the protected circumstances of their lives which distinguishes saints from ordinary people. They are not privileged people living aerated sanitised lives wherein God calls to them politely like an Anglican vicar in pure unaccented English; people who don't burp, who kneel and worship decorously without too much unseemly enthusiasm. But nor are they those who venerate enthusiasm to the extent that they exclude wisdom. Rowan Williams says: "John's poems are not emotional outpourings but theological statements of depth and seriousness." Those who have been honed by pain and by the awful reality of suffering rarely chase after false gods.

The saints are those who know what hell is like and, because they do, and because they are confined and constricted by suffering, the channels of their awareness of God deepen and they explode upwards into the sun, into the ray of darkness which John talks about like dolphins diving first into the depths of the sea and then leaping out from it into the light – a different breed from that growing in the rarefied comforts of the hothouse. John was never a hothouse religious. He must have known hell as well as heaven.

Not all those who suffer pain are honed by it, sharpened and strengthened. Some are destroyed. But, again, I believe strongly that we should learn about God from the study of physiology. I believe that God is merciful. When pain becomes too intense to bear we either lose consciousness or we die. Some die earlier than they should not from pain or disease but from fear itself. From Panic.

It is the learning how to bear pain which is so impor-

129

tant. And this is a process of learning. It doesn't come naturally. So much of what John is saying in the commentaries describes how to cope with pain and how necessary it is to cope with pain because pain is endemic in life.

But John was not a masochist. When, in the first pages of *The Ascent*, he describes the need to control the senses, to avoid anything "that is not purely for the honour and glory of God", he is talking about the pain of deprivation. But he makes it abundantly clear that this deprivation leads to very positive benefits – "put into practice, these maxims will give rise to abundant merit and great virtues", and, in the verses on page 103 of *The Ascent*, he always begins with the positive benefits:

... to reach satisfaction in all
desire its possession in nothing.
To come to possess all
desire the possession of nothing.

You cannot reach the top of a mountain without first climbing up the steep sides, without puffing and panting, without aches and pains. John's eye was always at the top of the mountain and he rattles on about the aches and pains but they are never an end in themselves; they are never self-punishment; they are a means of progress.

We are now in the midst of a reaction, a swing against the excesses which a misunderstanding of John's teaching on pain contributed to; when religious suffered themselves and inflicted upon others pain for its own sake, thinking that suffering in itself had a value whereas it is the conquering of pain which has value. Since the advent of modern psychology where masochism and indeed most things are seen to derive from strange sexual urges anyone advocating the positive aspect of pain is suspect. We have been trained to think we must at all costs avoid pain. Given a headache, we take an aspirin; given emotional pain, we take tranquillisers. We train our children to become weeping wimps and we deny them the very things they need for spiritual progress.

There are three alternative ways of coping with pain. The first is to remove the source. If your hand is burning take it away from the fire. John, when the chance occurred, escaped. He did not remain in prison suffering for suffering's sake. He used his common sense – the sense we all have in common – and he got out of it.

When escape is impossible the most usual reaction to pain is to endure it – to grit your teeth, think of England, waiting for its end, virtually saying to God, "If this is your will at the moment, I'm afraid you've got it wrong. This suffering isn't right for me and I hope that after a while you'll realise that."

There is a distinction between enduring and accepting – the third alternative – which is acutely subtle both to experience and to understand. The experience of enduring is that of awaiting change and of expecting that change to come from outside. The pain will be removed by drugs, by the doctor, by one's jailers, by God. You wait, fighting the pain because you think that it is wrong, it shouldn't be happening. Your body then becomes tense and the production of endorphins, the God-sent relief, is inhibited. Your body should never become a battleground. One of the current therapies designed to help cancer patients concerns visualisation techniques. The patient is told to imagine sharks swimming around in his intestines seeking out the cancer cells to devour; or wolves preying on the rogue cells and fighting them.

I disagree with this. I think it is of the greatest importance for us to forgive our bodies, to rest in harmony with them. Like the prodigal son we should welcome back into the family of our being the bits of it which seem to have betrayed us. If we fear some part of our

131

body as a traitor we will be in a state of inner conflict, surrounding that part with a barrier of tension and immobility so that the healing power of breathing and the free flow of blood is restricted. I can think of few things more disgusting than imagining sharks or wolves or birds of prey cavorting around in my body.

A political prisoner from Chile told me that in order to survive her torture, she had to forgive her torturers. Irina Ratushinskaya, the Russian poetess released from prison after five years, wrote to me and said, "This is how we survived in the labour camps: by using methods of relaxation."

Accepting means that instead of pain being seen as an evil to be fought against, dreaded and feared in tension and despair, it is seen as an inevitable part of life itself. It is not a punishment sent from God to torment us. God is good. Enduring implies lack of trust in God. Accepting means total trust.

John makes this distinction after quoting Job in the *Spiritual Canticle*:

"Just as the servant desires the shade, and the day labourer waits for the end of his work, so I had empty months and I counted the nights wearisome for myself. If I lie down to sleep, I shall say: When will the day come that I might arise?

It is noteworthy that the prophet Job did not say that the hireling was awaiting the end of his labour but the end of his work, in order to indicate what we are explaining, that is, that the soul that loves does not await the end of her labour but the end of her work. Her work is to love, and of this work, love, she awaits the end, which is the perfection and completeness of it. Until this work is accomplished the soul is always in the condition of the picture Job paints in this passage."

As soon as we learn to accept pain, to tolerate it – sometimes doctors get the use of words just right, and one of the definitions of the word 'tolerate' is 'forbearing to judge' – to see it as part of the work and to accept it, to stop fighting and to let go, we are pushed out from the dark bowels of discontent into the sun. The endorphin mechanism comes into play. We are not 'cured' in the sense that cancerous tissue falls away or the wounds of surgery miraculously disappear but we are healed. We accept the labour and look forward to the end of the work. We are whole – spelt with a 'w' – in place, in harmony with ourselves and God.

One young girl, a mother, said to me on the afternoon she died, paralysed and totally invaded by cancer, "It is bliss", and her face *was* blissful. She was a TV personality and had been baptised into the Church that same week. She was leaving a distraught young husband and her two-year-old son Thomas. The great sadness of her dying was in leaving him to fend for himself in the world without her love and protection.

But the pattern of her life had changed since her illness. Without it Thomas would have spent the first, the most formative years of his life, the years in which the battery of sensory impressions assaulting a baby at birth are conformed into order, in the care of a paid nanny so that his mother could continue her work. When she was ill she spent all day with him, loving him, caring for him in a way no paid person could share. I went to her room a few days before she died and she was lying in bed holding Thomas in her arms and they were both deeply, blissfully asleep. No child could want for more. No matter what the world may hold for Thomas he has had a gift from his mother which few of us can share. This was poetry. John had no child to hold in his arms while he suffered, so he wrote what he learned out for us, his spiritual children, for the generations who have lived after and learned from him.

John's poetry is not descriptive. It is explosive – like creation. The child when it is born is propelled from the womb, breaking through from the constriction which has held and protected him before birth, pushing his way out into the world until at last he is free. John called the freedom he reached in his prison cell 'the royal freedom of the spirit'. Those who reach this freedom, who suffer on the way, those are the fortunates. Forgive me but I must quote from Eckhart here. I find Eckhart and John have so much in common. "A life of rest and peace in God is good; a life of pain in patience is better; but to have peace in a life of pain is best of all."

John says:

Even though this happy night darkens the spirit, it does so only to impart light concerning all things; and even though it humbles a person and reveals his miseries, it does so only to exalt him; and even though it impoverishes and empties him of all possessions and natural affection, it does so only that he may reach out divinely to the enjoyment of all earthly and heavenly things, with a general freedom of spirit in them all.

But, as in all good things, there is a paradox. John started to write his poetry in prison. He says how releasing it is to suffer. But he escaped. You can't cheat with pain and suffering. If it is self-inflicted; if you make a voluntary choice to suffer for its own sake without keeping your sights on the mountain top, on progress towards God, you won't reach the royal realm of freedom. You will just suffer.

So John did not sit on in prison saying, "Thank you, God, for this lovely releasing pain." When he saw the chance of freeing himself he took it. He accepted his suffering, reached his royal freedom and escaped. And, by the way, that escape must have taken enormous courage. Prison can become a home. Stasis, even in prison, becomes preferable to change. Freedom can become the last, the most threatening thing you could want.

And change itself can be painful. Each religious order lays emphasis on certain aspects of spiritual development – no one can embrace them all. I am a lay Dominican, and one of the aspects of Dominican life which I respect is the lack of stasis. Dominicans move from place to place, from one relationship to another. They go at the demand of their superiors to wherever them may be sent. And in that continuous movement one finds a sense of permanence, of stability. You meet a fellow Dominican after many years of absence and you find nothing has changed between you. The transition from prison life to being back in his community must have been difficult for John. In prison he could not move. He could not divert himself by reading each new holy book which came on the market or by listening to each holy thought emanating from heads other than his own. Being alone with no diversion, his only book, the Scripture – not someone else's thoughts about the scriptures but the Scripture itself – is like a river which, from its source in the mountains, follows a deep channel growing in power and speed till it reaches the sea, where diversity causes the channel to become shallow, spreading out in little streams over the land, maybe puttering out altogether before it reaches its end. When John escaped from the big pain of imprisonment he had then to cope with the smaller pains of ordinary life again.

We learn from acute pain but the danger of Lilliputian pain is that it can make us stagnate. Often it isn't the deep experience, the great suffering that turns us away from God. Often it isn't the dramatic adultery that causes the break-up of a marriage. The rot may start in a marriage when one of the two can no longer stand the way in which the other eats corn flakes.

It is often the little suffering which turns us away; the small arrows continuously bombarding us, bitchiness rather than open cruelty; discomfort rather than acute pain; mediocrity rather than intensity.

John was grateful for his intense pain because it made him react with intensity; grateful to God for sending him suffering. And we should be too if it comes to us, because then we are forced to grow in order to survive. If we reject pain, it destroys us. We have to learn to accept, even to welcome it, for it is our teacher – often the only way open to us to learn, giving us the impetus to change not the outside things but ourselves and our way of reacting to them. But – we cannot cheat. The life of the ascetic, busy in self-condemned squalor, *may* lead to John's royal freedom of the spirit or it may lead to spiritual autotomy. If you don't recognise the word neither did I until I was researching in a medical library. It is the disease of eating oneself. Chewing the extremities until they are gnawed down to the knuckle. Obsessive concern with self-inflicted pain is like spiritual autotomy. Rather than reach out towards freedom you chew bits of yourself out of existence. The chewed hand or foot is no longer there, but where is it? John, when he could, escaped. He learned from pain inflicted not by himself but by his brethren. And then he escaped. Like the flower growing out of the concrete which then sows its seeds in the fertile ground nearby, he went on writing poetry.

Iain Matthew

John and daily life

Most of us experience life, most of the time, as ordinary and sometimes even boring. There appears a depressing distance between Gospel ideals and the imprisoning mediocrity of daily life. Iain Matthew asks the question: does John of the Cross have anything to say to us whose lives are, at best, average. The answer is yes.

A young girl in Avila, wealthy and easy-going, had come to feel (or friends had come to feel) that she should take the gospel more seriously. "There's a confessor at the convent of the Incarnation just outside the city walls – why not go to him?" "What, him?! He's supposed to be a saint; what are you trying to make me?" Despite her inhibitions, the girl did find herself, resistant but resigned, in front of Fray Juan de la Cruz. His holiness was at once a challenge and a barrier. Better, surely, to be ordinary and live, than to break under the pressure of ideals that real life cannot support.

The encounter points up a wider difficulty: the depressing distance between Gospel ideals and the imprisoning mediocrity of daily life. Its routine remains, and hammers home the conviction that God, for all the Church's eloquence, lies beyond our grasp. The climb is too exacting. Life leaves no space for it.

Juan's genius is at home in crisis (1N 8.3); when the journey turns *al revés*, back to front, his pen drips gold. But does he have anything to say to life as daily, as ordinary – even as boring?

In seeking an answer, we shall attempt, not so much to suggest practical ways of coping with his counsels as to penetrate to the point where Juan's writing and his own life are one; from there he speaks to us a seminal word; and we shall find that word confronting, inevitably, our practical lives. First, then, does he write from life and for life? His response to the girl from Avila is encouraging:

> I'm not a saint; but you should realise that the holier a confessor is, the gentler he'll be, and the less he'll be shocked at others' faults; for he knows better how weak people are.[1]

Except when he is apologising (2A 14.14) or carried away by conviction (F 3.27), Juan scarcely uses the word 'I'. While Teresa's writings reverberate with her presence, Juan is a master at self-concealment. One can wonder whether his writings have much to do with him at all.

It is certain that life, more than books, furnished Juan with his most formative schooling. To mention two periods marked by the mixture of pain and warmth characterising his entire life: his childhood saw his widowed mother earn the family's bread at the cost of raw fingers and heartache, but encouraging the boys to share that bread with villagers poorer than they. Her motto: "Don't eat without sharing." Again, Juan's teens exposed him to life's open wounds as he daily attended people dying of venereal syphilis in the *Hospital de las bubas*, yet Juan retained the level-headedness to study and light-heartedness to entertain even in that atmosphere.[2]

As a friar, Juan continued living close to soil and suffering. His first commitment was to the life of his community. His days were filled too with gardening, brick-laying, journeying around Andalusia in administrative business; only lastly, and reluctantly, with writing mystical prose.[3]

Yet when we ask for a word about daily life he is not going to tell us about nursing, gardening or administration – nor directly about politics, sociology, even psychology. His contribution will tell us about God. There people found his own approach fresh. To quote his

140

secretary and close friend: "God was his constant theme: ... and he spoke of him so attractively... that he made us all laugh and we'd go out very happy."[4]

Juan speaks about God. His word is *from life* not because it relates routine realities but because it issues from source, from the raw nerve that lies beneath the surface. It took human and divine surgery to expose that nerve. His Toledo prison offered the theatre.

In 1577 Juan was halfway through his life as a friar; he had studied, prayed, taught faithfully. Yet now in his dungeon he had an experience of discipleship that crossed new frontiers. Physically, through malnutrition, torture, squalor, his survival was set in the balance. Emotionally, his captivity induced in him a fear of death, a threatening sense of failure, and the loneliness implicit in his anxiety that Teresa and the others would consider he had deserted them.[5] As for his relationship with God, while testimonies are scarce, they weigh heavily: "During the time they had him in prison, he suffered great inner affliction and aridity" (Inocencio de San Andrés[6]); at times the Lord "abandoned him, and left him in an inner darkness as great as the darkness of his cell" (the nuns at Sabiote).[7]

Here Juan cried out a question. *Adónde te escondiste Amado...?* "Where have you hidden, Beloved...?" These are the first words of the 'Canticle', composed by Juan in Toledo. They convey the anxiety of one who had lived, taught, worshipped in the sunlight of God all his life, but who now, in this darkness, needed to meet him.

Dungeon, prison, is an image Juan employs in *Night* to convey the experience of purgation (2N 1,1; 7.3,4); it seems he employs it because prison is where Juan himself traversed the "cruel death of the spirit" (2N 6.1). But this death provided space, space for "the longed – for resurrection" (ibid.). Night is an experience of the sign of Jonah (2N 6.1,3); and Juan qualifies Toledo as his own entombment in the sea-beast (Lt 1). It was for him not a disaster but a pasch: a poverty that allowed a new, a deeper communion.

Something was released in Juan there that issued in the poems for which he is famous. We know that in prison he composed the first 31 stanzas of the *Canticle*, the *Romances* on the Incarnation, and the *Fountain* which flows by night. Of the *'Canticle'* Juan testifies that it was the fruit not just of artistic skill but of encounter with his beloved – born of "love in mystical understanding" (CP I). In the *'Romances'* the identity of the beloved stands revealed: the Jesus of Bethlehem and Calvary, whose way it is to come to meet the poor – those drowning in 'the lake' – and to raise them with him to the Father by first drowning with them (R 7.264-265).

Juan's emptying in Toledo made room for Christ. This presence was known as from behind, from within: "Amid these dark pains" there emerges "a certain companionship and inner strength walking with her" (2N 11.7). Night acclimatised Juan to one who had long been present – as one may see a silhouette in a darkened room, once the eyes have grown used to the obscurity. Night made Juan the poor man who could know Christ's unpaid-for desire to love him – a companionship that is new, original, outside any anticipation, personal.

This episode can be seen as the womb forming Juan's entire doctrine: the ever-present Christ presses to befriend; poverty, nakedness, *nada* , function only to allow the gift. And all Juan's writing takes us back to that reality of his own encounter with the beloved: the prose explains the poverty; the poetry emerges from the experience; prose, poetry, experience are a single thread leading us to the inner sanctuary of Juan's communion with the living God.

That is an extraordinary privilege. Juan, the quiet author, in fact entrusts to us his very heart-beat. His writing is indeed *from* life – almost too closely, too uncensored.

Juan speaks for life

Much of Juan's writing envisages religious like himself. *Ascent* is especially for "friars and nuns" of "our sacred Order" (A P 9); *Canticle* addresses *Ana de Jesús*, prioress in Granada (C title; P 3). On the other hand, the *Flame*, the work dearest to Juan, is dedicated to *Ana de Penalosa*, a lay woman, a close friend; and Juan's correspondents include people from different walks of life, to whom he proposes the same kind of doctrine as that addressed to religious in the longer writings.

More than a particular state of life, Juan focuses on a particular stage of growth. His concern is prayer beyond the beginnings – not because the beginnings are unimportant but because others had written to them amply, and because his immediate addressees were being led to a deeper form of communion (CP 3). In practice, Juan concentrates his energy on contemplative prayer, where former gratification dries up, because God is engaging the person at a deeper level (AP 3; 2A 11-15; 1N 8-10; F 3.32-43). Juan offers teaching here which he acknowledges would harm people whose lives are following a different tack (3A 2.1).

Yet given this focus, Juan is concerned to shed the light he finds there on Christians at *every* stage of the journey. His vision is secure, and from it he can throw life-lines. Hence in *Canticle*, though he is not very consistent, yet he does begin his commentary by applying the opening stanza to people like the girl in Avila, once she had nerved herself to a more serious following of Jesus (CB *Argumento*; CB 1.1). In *Flame*, he regards God's purifying work to be active not only in contemplatives, but through the difficulties and disappointments that "ordinarily and humanly happen to *all that live*" (LB 2.27).

Juan is not exclusive. On the contrary, he, supposedly the great systematiser, is more characteristically the champion of each person's uniqueness. "God leads each person by a different path, so that, in even half her approach, you'll hardly find a single person following the same route as another" (LB 3.59). This respect for the individual dictated Juan's pastoral approach. The disordered sisters at the Incarnation, nervous of their new director, were "struck by his great patience":

> He bore their imperfections, however many times he might point them out, and he led them forward, at their own imperfect pace, to perfection, without violence, and by weak means led them to strength – and by this mildness and prudent patience he obliged them more than ever.[8]

Part of the beauty of creation that Juan relishes is its 'harmony'.[9] That harmony includes the gradualness with which the person becomes what God intends her to be. For Juan, God acts respectfully, "with order, gentleness, and in a way that suits the soul" (2A 17.3). On the cross, Jesus wrought the cosmic espousal of mankind with God which becomes ours in Baptism. The protracted journey to union with God of which Juan writes in *Canticle* is, he tells us, the same espousal; but the former (cross/sacraments) happened "at God's pace" – "all at once"; life works the espousal "at the soul's pace", and so "little by little" (C 23.6). Wherever the unfolding may have reached in our own case, we may presume on Juan's respect, and trust the sunlight blazing on him to refract back to us gently enough not to be destructive.

Yet while he is sensitive, he is uncompromising in his summons. The goal he holds out is 'union' – a word selected carefully (A title: AP 1; 2A 5); it signifies not a Promethean magnitude but personal communion with Christ the beloved (1A 14.2; 1N 1.2; 2N 24.3). This he regards as the only legitimate fulfilment for the human person: "for *this* goal of love were we created" (C 29.3).

It is a goal that God wishes "all people" to reach (F2.27). And Juan holds it out as a real possibility, so real for Juan that people's reluctance to grasp the hour of grace draws from him his most impassioned pleas: *"Oh almas criadas para estas grandezas...!"* "Oh souls created for this greatness and summoned to it! What are you doing?" (C 39.7; cf 1A 5.4; F 2.28). This is the second flame in Juan's writing. His poetry emerged from the Spirit-fire of his experience; his pastoral anxiety flares up as he sees the potential of the reader.

Juan, living in a age over-stuffed with religiosity, has a clear intention not to add but to deepen. He is pained to see people who "wear themselves out with exertion, and in fact head backwards, thinking that they'll make progress in what is no help at all" (AP 7); if people who load themselves with extraordinary practices put "half as much effort" into what actually profits, they would advance further "in one month" than they will as things stand "in many years" (1A 8.4). He is convinced: union with God in love is a real possibility for each person. Nothing must prevent it. Where union with Christ is at stake, 'This doesn't apply to me,' is not, in Juan's view, a legitimate response.

What, then, excludes us from his writing? It is not our particular state of life (secular, religious, married or single); nor is it exactly our stage of growth or manner of prayer; rather, it is unwillingness to be changed. Juan demands of us desire: "what prepares a person to be united with God is the desire for God" (F 3.26). Yet this must be, not a vapid wishfulness, but a desire prepared to see the costly work wrought within (cf F 2.27); and the password into the sanctuary is a shared question" "Where have you hidden?"

Juan's discovery: God presses in to give himself

If we come to Juan seeking *God* in our daily lives, then he has an answer. It comes to us first as his testimony to what God has done for him. He discloses it most powerfully in the *Flame*. This was the work dearest to Juan: in it, he claims, experience, poetry, prose, each issue from the action within him of the Spirit of Jesus, *el Espiritu de su Esposo* (F 1.3; cf FP 1). Juan was so concerned to get it right that he set himself to re-edit the work in his final months, even though he discovered little that needed changing. He bequeathed a copy of it to his surgeon, Dr Villareal, shortly before he died. It is like his last testament, signed in God's presence.

> Flame, white-hot and compelling,
> yet tender past all telling,
> reaching the secret centre of my soul!
> Since now evasion's over,
> finish your work, my Lover,
> break the last thread, wound me and make me whole!

> Oh llama de amor viva
> que tiernamente hieres
> de mi alma en el más profundo centro!
> Pues ya no eres esquiva,
> acaba ya si quieres:
> rompe la tela de este dulce encuentro!

This 'testament' tells us of the action, within Juan, of Another – of the fire that surrounds and invades. This is Juan's definitive word about God: he is not passive; he transforms. And the message reverberates through the prose, which so echoes the poem in its imagery and cadence that it is like an extension of the stanzas – a world of uncontainable vitality, irrepressible as fire, since "love is never idle, but in continuous movement" (F

1.8). Here Juan exposes to us his communion with God traced to source, a genuine theology, telling us what the God we know from revelation does to a person who takes him seriously. Juan tells us: God answers the person's deepest need. He communicates himself, not some substitute – some idea, or feeling, or assurance – but himself, personally. In the *Flame* the bride "tastes the living God" because he "communicates himself" (F 1.6). This is no general gift, but one made to the person as if the unique object of God's love, it seems to her that "he is all for her alone" (F 2.36). And the only explanation for this gift is the God who gives it: "there is no need to question in astonishment" (FP 2), since "when one person loves another... he loves her according to his own personality and characteristics; just so your bridegroom, who dwells within you, *as he who he is* shows you favour" (F 3.6; cf FP 2). Juan thus becomes like wax supple to God's impression (cf C 12.1). And the divine protagonist is known to be never stale but "always new" (F 2.36); the Spirit's presence is a *"fiesta"* (ibid.).

Juan bequeaths, then, the impress of God. At the same time the flame lights up Juan's own capacity – the F*lame* thus gives us, too, a true anthropology. Albeit 'little by little', God's love capacitates the person to receive his gift. "He loves you, making you equal to himself" Juan is bold enough to say (F 3.6). Juan can speak to the 'caverns' of his own spirit as infinite, "since what can fill them is infinite – and that is God" (F 3.22). Only from this perspective can we value the human person as he or she is worth. "A single thought of man is worth more than all the world; only God is worthy of it" (SLL 34).

From this Juan can answer his own question: Will God fill me or destroy me? *"El fin de Dios es engrandecer laalma"*, "God's purpose is to make the person great"(F 2.3).

Juan's discovery is for us

The word issuing from Juan's exposure to the living God is our word. Juan's God is always self-bestowing: manifestly and joyfully at the end of the journey, but throughout the journey still the flame that invades, the "principal lover", "principal agent, guide and motive force" who infallibly precedes us in initiative (C 31.8; F 3.46: C 32.5; cf F 1.19).

Juan is perhaps most widely known for his teaching on God-given 'contemplation', and the 'dark night' pain that heralds it. But prior to any practical help that teaching may offer to anyone going through the darkness, Juan by it makes two universal statements about God: God is an inflowing God; and his inflow transforms.

'Contemplation' is, in Juan's understanding, that inflow engaging the person even psychologically; and the change wrought in the 'night' is particularly dramatic. But Juan's doctrine here as it were captures in still photography a key moment in what is a continuing process. God was still inflowing prior to this psychological engagement, inflaming the bride with love from the first so that she might be able to make the first steps towards him: *"en amores inflamada"*, "with love inflamed", 1A 14.2; cf 1.4); and "the loving mother of the grace of God" was working change in the person even in the first fervour of conversion (1N 1.2; 8.3). Hence from the summit Juan can proclaim, "God is always like that, as the soul now sees him to be: moving, ruling, giving being and strength and graces and gifts to all his creatures" (F4.7).

We may offer three illustrations of this.

Firstly, God's self-bestowal is made irreversibly in Jesus. He for Juan is the *todo*, the all, for which negation, *nada*, makes space (2A 22.4). Jesus' crucifixion is Juan's guarantee. There God and humanity became indissolubly one (CB 23.3-5). Juan prays:

You will not take from me, my God, what you once gave me in your only Son, Jesus Christ (Prayer of a soul in love).

But on that basis Juan recognises God's surrounding readiness as a constant reality:

"... hence I rejoice that if I hope, you will not delay..."

Juan understands the risen Jesus as one whose nearness is not sealed up; it seeps through to hesitant hearts – as he "inflamed the heart in faith" on the road to Emmaus, or instructed Mary Magdalen "with the warmth of his presence" (3S 31.8).

Again, in the language of *Canticle*, God is accompanying us, penetrating us with his gaze: the bride feels he is "always gazing upon her" (C11.4); and for him "to gaze" means 'to love' (C19.6), "to love first" (C31.8). This gaze *does* things: it cleanses, enriches, sheds light, imparts beauty (C33.1). God thus commits himself to escalating payments, since each look of his makes the bride more loveable: "When you gazed on me, your gaze set deep your beauty in my heart; for this you loved me more..." (C stz 32). And for God to love means not simply to admire or to wish well but (an extraordinary statement) to take us into himself so that he can love us as himself (C32.6). God's impressing gift, where received, will never leave the person as she was.

Matters come to a head in the *Flame*. Juan is to lean back from his own communion with God to recover the reader. He does not really want to interrupt the flow; but he is compelled to do so by the deep sorrow he feels (*"mancilla y lástima"*) at seeing people ignore God's invitation. In this context he magisterially asserts: "Because it is so necessary, not only for these people who are doing so well, but for all those who are looking for their beloved..." What he is about to say is addressed, then, to all those who can share his question. Where have you hidden? To these he proclaims:

> The first thing you should realise is that if the person is seeking God, much more is her beloved seeking her (LB 3.28).

God: constantly hungering; inflowing and transforming.

Juan's word and daily life

What is the relevance of this for daily life? Juan has here filled in no details about the steps we are to take in discipleship; no exercises; no programmes. His contribution goes further. He tells us God's reality for *us* : God holds us in a gaze that offers us nothing less than himself. Already the message of that love releases us from paralysis. When a person knows herself loved, that makes her capable of sacrifice and generosity. As Teresa was to say, Juan's gift to the Church is the fact, realised in him, of God's self-giving nearness. Knowing that this is our environment, we can make the first step which previously our sense of impotence had paralysed us into refusing. The Avila girl, once she heard Juan's gentle understanding, could begin the conversion no amount of cajoling could have wrested from her.

Juan's word thus confers our true context; it also rephrases the question. No longer is the task to crawl out of life's greyness up to a passively waiting God. It is rather to receive the one who tenders himself to us in ever-pressing nearness. That changes everything. And Juan's every word makes sense in this light. *Nada* becomes a word of delight – a word of hands "free" to receive "such fair and wholesome freedom" (Lt 7). Juan's ministry becomes a mission to elicit openness to God's invasion. Leonor was sad at leaving a loved community. Juan is genuinely sympathetic. But (with a mesmeric turn of phrases) he considers that God is using the very human circumstance to make space in her heart, so that his gift of himself – always tendered – may more effectively impinge: "For this reason, he would love to see you, since he loves you well, well and truly alone, intent on being himself all your company" (Lt 15). Again, in Juan's own most bitter hour, when even the friars of the reform had turned against him, and those who stayed with him could not tolerate the injustice, Juan could react like Jesus because he received his response from him:

> Love greatly those who contradict you and do not love you, because that way you'll elicit love in a heart that has none. That's what God does with us: he loves us, that we may love him through the love in which he holds us (Lt 33).

This vision of God's self-bestowing nearness makes sense also of the leitmotif of Juan's writings: his insistence on faith, hope, love, as the only means that will offer the direct personal union with God he seeks.

Faith, hope, love: God communicating himself to the soul

Juan at last has an answer to the question, ¿*Adónde.? Where can I find him?*

> ... If you want to hear it again, listen to a word filled with reality and unfathomable truth. It is this: seek him, in faith and love (C 1.11).

Faith and love answer Juan's search for encounter with God himself. They mean, not launching out on an

151

unrealisable quest but opening to the one who presses in to give himself. God, Juan asserts, is the centre of the soul, present to her there where she is most herself, beyond concept, beyond feeling (C1.4-7). There he tenders his friendship and, through Baptism, capacitates her to receive it. Attending to, desiring the God proposed in Jesus (faith, hope, love) draws us to that "centre" and makes us "one with him" (F 1.12-13). While Juan sets his sights on the full flowering of love, he states that the least degree of such love effects the longed-for union. There is here no excuse for delay.

At first Juan's emphasis in treating of these theological virtues seems curiously negative: don't let any other meaning be your security, don't set your heart on any other attraction – 2 and 3 *Ascent* list these potential alternatives, insisting, "Not this"; "Well, surely this?"; "Sorry, not that either." The master class goes on relentlessly. But Juan's negativity, destructive if left in itself, makes sense because for him God's truth and love are realities that invade. Faith and love are firstly God giving himself to us, only secondarily our response. So of faith, Juan writes, that it is dark because it is "light too bright"; it is light which is "God communicating himself to the soul" (2A 9.1-3). Faith is dark not because distant but because God is there immediately close, inside the limit of our focus

Here above all, then, Juan's negativity is a receptivity. The active aspect of faith, hope, love is a 'making space' for a gift immediate in its nearness, like water pressing up against a dam: "making space for God in order to receive" (F 2.27); "when the soul gives room for God, then she is enlightened and transformed in God" (2A 5.7). Only because of this can Juan say that one act of unsullied love is worth more than all the other works, tinged with self, we can perform (C 29.1): because in love, theological love, the world receives God.

Juan therefore makes a promise. Where faith, hope

and love do their self-stripping, Christ-attending work, there the person lives her own Toledo: in her poverty, God discovers her.

If in this way you empty the soul of everything, so that she becomes free in their regard, which is what the soul can do on her part, it is impossible that God fail to play his part, by communicating himself, at least in a hidden way (F 3.46).

For Juan, faith, hope and love in act are prayer: opening to the one whose immediate presence is always held out to us. "Enter within your heart, and work in the presence of your Spouse, who is always present, loving you well" (SLL 89). God's nearness means two things. It means that prayer is possible, always – even in ordinariness. It means also that it will be hidden in faith, not exposed in sight or feeling. Juan sets out the programme:

> Find joy, find contentment there, gathered together and given to him who dwells within, since he is so close to you; desire him there, adore him there, and don't go off looking for him anywhere else... There's only one problem. Even though he is within you, he is hidden (C 1.17).

Juan can reduce prayer to a simple formula: "... your concern must be to be with God within" (C 1.10; cf 3A 42.2). 'Within': the home of expectancy; there where we can devote ourselves entirely, where the person is not fragmented. 'To be with': an attentive presence, larger than words or images (though those may support it, 2A 14.2); perhaps silent, but the silence that will allow the Father to "speak" Jesus Christ, his "only word", with unrestricted volume (2A 22; SLL 99). 'With God'; the God whose gift, made ours in Bethlehem, on Calvary, is ceaselessly tendered; a God with whom we can 'be' only because he has elected to 'be with' us.

153

Daily life: an obstacle

Where the issue of God's gift of himself from within, the ordinariness of life should be at least irrelevant. We shall find it a bonus. But first there are two ways in which it can be an obstacle.

Poetry answers Juan's need because it communicates more than the bare words define. Constantly, Juan is up against the impotence of language – so much so that the first version of the *Flame* ended abruptly: "The Holy Spirit filled her with goodness and glory, winning her to a love beyond language, beyond feeling, wresting her to the depths of God. So, I stop here. *Finis*" (F 4.17). It is proof of Juan's having 'been there', that, despite his inability to describe, he still appeals: Please believe me...

> I've no doubt that some people not understanding this nor knowing it by experience, will either disbelieve it or think it exaggerated, or reckon it less than it in fact is. But to all of these I answer, that the Father of lights, who bestows himself abundantly wherever he finds room, like a ray of sunlight, ... does not hesitate to find his delight in the company of the sons of men (F 1.15).

Against this, life's ordinariness invites disbelief. 'Nothing ever happens, or at least not to me.' It invites it the more so in a society taught to see greatness in the spectacular, and to need novelty. In such an atmosphere, Juan's promise is demanding. He asks us to believe that God is answering our deepest longing; that he gives himself; and that that gift transcends the level of feeling to which we are accustomed. Against the minimalism of daily life, which reads poetry as just bad prose, Juan demands resurrection faith – belief issuing in desire:

... You show yourself first, and you come out to meet *those who desire you* (SLL 2).

That is one obstacle: the inclination to disbelief. The other is the temptation to escape life's ordinariness by a round of evasion, diversion, addiction – the seductive lure of superficial gratification. Juan recognises that we become as big or as small as what we set our heart on (1A 4.8). Such attachment tragically narrows the heart and makes it incapable of the life it pretends to offer. "The person has only one will, and if this gets caught up in a particular thing it won't be free, it won't be complete, single or pure – yet that's what's needed if God is to transform us" (1A 11.6). Juan paints a devastating portrait of the person bound by ambition: "their concerns deprive them of all vitality, eaten up with care and a whole lot of misery, not allowing joy to enter their hearts..." (3A 19.10). This pained inertia is not the stillness Juan would wish for us, and here he does invite a gesture – the kind of gesture that strikes at the root and really profits. He invites us to 'go out'; to move, not so much dramatically – perhaps into some other state of life, where more seems to be 'happening' – but constructively, out of our paralysis. Leave the prison of sensuality and egoism – this is Juan's programme of negation, a saying 'No' to what enslaves, that our hands may be free for what fulfils (Lt 5; cf 3A 17.2). On occasion (when appropriate, 1A 13.4), step out of what seems like necessity. 'I don't need that; I need God.' Juan's invitation to self-transcendence targets first the root of sin, and his suggestions are practicable: do something kind without looking for acknowledgement (3A 28); stand back from petty politicking (*Precautions* 12); don't require respect and attention (C 28.7); or, the gesture pre-eminent in Juan's own life, forgive.

Daily life: the opportunity

Belief, desire, a gesture to cut loose from the web of evasion: these allow daily life to do the work for which it was intended. In its ordinariness, when it is boring, it offers of itself a kind of *vacio*, emptiness. This can be for Juan the condition for the greatest fullness.

Juan is opposed to interior nomadism – the indecision of people governed by superficial gratification. "They spend their lives changing vocations, changing approaches." Juan opposes this fickleness to 'poverty', to 'silence'. It is these that penetrate to reality, to what is really life – to *lo vivo, las sustancia, las verdad* (1N 3.1; 3A 41.1-2; F3.34). Juan asks us not to evade life's ordinariness but to allow God to unlock us through it:

> So then: when gratification is wrested from you, don't let this cause you pain; instead consider it a great blessing; because God is freeing you from yourself (2N 16.8).

Being content to 'be with God within' in this atmosphere, beyond gratification and feeling: this for Juan opens us to real newness – not the novelty of news and fashion, but the newness of another person, whose love is always unpaid for and original.

Life's ordinariness gives space – *vacio* – precisely for that gift, if we are prepared, daily, to meet God's gaze in faith. "Let her not fail to pray, and let her hope, for he who is good to her will not delay" (*no tardará su bien*, 3A 3.6).

Life's ordinariness can allow Juan's cry: Where have you hidden? to be heard; it can allow God's answer, his gift of himself, to rise at the source of the question.

Believe in the gift.

Do not seek to escape the stillness.

Attend in love to him who is present, communicating himself.

Juan prays:

Do you awaken us, my Lord, and shed your light upon us, that we might recognise and come to love the blessings that you always hold out to us. And we shall realise that you stepped forward to show us your favour, and that you have not forgotten us (F 4.9).

NOTES

1. Interpreting Ms 19407 ff, 151, Crisógono, *Vida de San Juan de la Cruz*, Madrid 1982, p. 117.
2. So Jerónimo de San José, *Historia* (Madrid 1641), Hardy, *The Life of St John of the Cross*, London 1982, p. 14.
3. Juan's reluctance to write is evident in FP 1; and in the unfinished state of *Ascent* – composed intermittently – and *Night*.
4. Juan Evangelista, Juan's friend, secretary, confessor. Ms 12738 ff, 560, Crisógono, p. 413 n. 33.
5. The testimonies are collected in Pacho, *Los Escritos de San Juan de la Cruz*, Madrid 1969, pp. 99-122.
6. Inocencio is one of the most reliable witnesses to the prison events and Juan's reactions. Ms 8568 fol. 544, Crisógono, p. 156 n. 49.
7. Ms 12738 p. 22; Pacho, p. 111.
8. Quiroga, *Historia*, Brussels 1628, I, 48, 194 – resuming the testimony of those involved.
9. C 14/15.4; 16.10; F 3.7.

The translation of stz 1 of the *Flame* is by Marjorie Flower OCD, Adelaide 1983. Other translations of Juan's text are mine. Some ideas in this paper derive from those of Federico Ruiz OCD and Maximiliano Herráiz OCD.